Lecture Notes
in Economics and
Mathematical Systems
Managing Editors: M. Beckmann and H. P. Künzi

Economic Theory

176

Rolf Färe

Dear Professor Shephard,

Many thanks for all you have tought me

Rolf

Laws of Diminishing Returns

Springer-Verlag
Berlin Heidelberg New York 1980

Managing Editors

Prof. Dr. M. Beckmann
Brown University
Providence, RI 02912/USA

Prof. Dr. H. P. Künzi
Universität Zürich
CH-8090 Zürich/Schweiz

Author

Rolf Färe
Department of Economics
Southern Illinois University
Carbondale, IL 62901/USA

ISBN 3-540-09744-9 Springer-Verlag Berlin Heidelberg New York
ISBN 0-387-09744-9 Springer-Verlag New York Heidelberg Berlin

Library of Congress Cataloging in Publication Data
Färe, Rolf, 1942-
Laws of diminishing returns.
(Lecture notes in economics and mathematical systems; 176)
Bibliography: p.
Includes index.
1. Diminishing returns. I. Title. II. Series.
HB241.F33 338.5'12 80-417
ISBN 0-387-09744-9

Printing and binding: Beltz Offsetdruck, Hemsbach/Bergstr.
2141/3140-543210

To

Carolina and Inger

PREFACE

Diminishing Returns is a concept deeply rooted in economic thought. After being introduced by Turgot in 1767 it has become accepted as one of the cornerstones of contemporary economic theory.

My interest in this area started in the fall semester of 1971 at U.C. Berkeley where I was enrolled in Professor Ronald W. Shephard's class on the theory of production. Shephard introduced me to his work on the Law of Diminishing Returns, and encouraged me to continue that work. This monograph is a result of my inspiring experience with Professor Shephard; and I am sincerely grateful to him for everything he has taught me.

In developing some of the materials in this monograph I have collaborated with my Swedish friends Leif Jansson and Leif Svensson. It has been a pleasure to work with such capable individuals.

For reading and making suggestions on a preliminary version of the monograph, thanks are due to W. Eichhorn, R. Kirk and R. Sato, and of course to my SIU friends Shawna Grosskopf and Dan Primont.

I would also like to gratefully acknowledge the support received from a Stiftelsen Siamon grant.

Last but not least, special thanks are given to Claudia Striegel for her care and patience in typing this manuscript.

Rolf Färe

October, 1979

Carbondale, Illinois

TABLE OF CONTENTS

1. DIMINISHING RETURNS

1.1 Introduction

Economists distinguish between laws of diminishing returns at the extensive margin, (Steuart) and at the intensive margin, (Turgot). Steuart (1767) argued that as additional land was opened up for agricultural production, the quality of the soil declined and proportionally more land had to be used as input for proportional increases in yields.

At the intensive margin, Turgot (1767) introduced into economic thought the proposition that as equal quantities of capital and labor are applied successively to a given plot of land, the output resulting from these applications will increase monotonically up to a certain point, after which further application will result in steadily decreasing product increments tending to zero. This proposition prompted Schumpeter (1966) to state: "It embodies an achievement that is nothing short of brilliant and suffices in itself to place Turgot as a theorist high above Adam Smith."

Although the original spirit of diminishing returns concerned the constraint to agricultural yields imposed by the scarcity of land, adaptation of diminishing returns to modern production technologies is even more important. What appears obvious for land is more subtle in the case of a modern production technology with substitution possibilities among numerous factors of production.

In today's world, limitations on natural resources present a problem for production. Some factors are substitutable, while others which may be essential for production are not substitutable. A modern formulation of the law of diminishing returns must deal with these problems. Therefore, precise definitions and rigorous tools must be applied.

In agriculture, transportation and engineering, diminishing returns and congestion are frequently observed making a theoretical understanding of these phenomena a most important prerequisite in the formulation of proper models for empirical investigations.

The classical attempts to deduce laws of diminishing returns from generally acceptable axioms of a production technology have been reviewed by Menger (1936). He concludes that they have been deficient in logic, tautological or contrived to obtain the desired result. It was not until Shephard (1970) published his article: "Proof of the Law of Diminishing Returns", in Zeitschrift für Nationalökonomie that one was able to deduce a law of diminishing returns from acceptable axioms of the production structure.

Shephard proved that if a proper subset of production factors is essential (in the sense that in their absence only null output is possible), then there exists a positive bound on these which constrains the output obtainable.

1.2 Restrictions of the Study

Throughout this monograph it is assumed that only one output is produced. This seemingly restrictive assumption is introduced mainly for pedagogical reasons. However, the use of production functions is a common practice in production theory and it is therefore important to discuss laws of diminishing returns within this framework. In addition, the subtlety and depth of these laws are such that there is some danger in presenting them in a more general context. On the other hand, some of the theorems in this monograph have been generalized to multiproduct technologies, see Shephard and Färe (1974).

A second restriction imposed throughout this study is that of a steady state. A production technology is considered to be in a steady state situation if the past and the future can be ignored. Output is immediately produced from inputs. The sausage machine can be thought of as an example. This restriction excludes time substitution and its effects. Since the mathematical tools needed to analyze these laws in a dynamic setting are tools that economists in general are not familiar with, I have chosen to work within a steady state framework. For the interested reader, dynamic laws are developed by Färe (1978), Shephard and Färe (1978).

1.3 Outline of the Monograph

The remainder of this monograph is divided into six chapters of which the last is a mathematical appendix. In Chapter 2 the theoretical framework for production used in this study is developed. It relates the input correspondence to the production function and contains theorems which are of importance for the ensuing analysis. Also, examples of specific production structures are introduced.

Chapter 3 develops the relationship between essential subsets of production factors and bounded output. By means of functional equation methods, conditions on the production function necessary and sufficient for bounded average returns are derived.

In Chapter 4, congestion and null jointness among inputs is discussed. These notions are used to prove necessary and sufficient conditions on the production structure for laws of variable proportions to prevail.

Chapter 5 develops the law of diminishing returns at the extensive margin. Conditions of the production function and the inputs are derived for this law to apply.

2. THE PRODUCTION TECHNOLOGY

2.1 Introduction

A production technology or a production structure specifies alternative ways of arranging means of production (inputs, factors of production) to obtain output. A production structure may be modelled by the input requirements for output or by the output yield from inputs, depending upon what is most appropriate. However, the two approaches are required to be consistent, since the conclusions should be independent of the approach.

In this monograph input requirements are modelled by an input correspondence which maps outputs into subsets of factors of production. Output is taken as a nonnegative scalar $u \varepsilon R_+$, and inputs as a nonnegative vector $x = (x_1, x_2, \ldots, x_n) \varepsilon R^n_+$. The approach based on output yield is modelled by a production function which maps input vectors into scalar outputs. This function is defined for each input vector as the maximum obtainable output.

It was not until Shephard (see Shephard, 1967 and 1970:a) showed that the production function and input correspondence approaches are equivalent that one obtained the foundation of production theory necessary for analyzing laws of bounded output and laws of diminishing returns. To make this monograph self-contained, the equivalence between the input correspondence and the production function is shown.

For an input correspondence or a production function to be an appropriate model of a production structure it has to satisfy certain properties, axioms. These production axioms and the relationship between the input correspondence and the production function are discussed in sections 2.2 and 2.3. The axioms in this monograph are weaker than those found in Shephard (1967) and (1970:a). They follow those of Shephard (1974). See also Färe (1972).

Basic properties of the production technology which satisfy the production axioms are proved in section 2.4. Some of these properties are of interest as independent results, while others are applied in later chapters. The last section in this chapter contains examples of specific production structures like homothetic, almost homothetic and WDI. These structures frequently appear later in this monograph.

2.2 The Input Correspondence

The production technology is modelled here by an input correspondence L, which maps outputs into subsets of inputs. Formally, $R_+ \ni u \to L(u) \varepsilon 2^{R^n_+}$, where $2^{R^n_+}$ denotes the set of subsets of R^n_+. The input set L(u) contains all input vectors $x \varepsilon R^n_+$ yielding output $u \varepsilon R_+$.

Two subsets of L(u) are important in the text, namely; the Isoquant (I(u)) and the Efficient subset (E(u)). These subsets are defined as:

$$(2.2.1) \quad \begin{cases} I(u) := \{x \varepsilon R^n_+ : x \varepsilon L(u),\ \lambda \cdot x \notin L(u) \text{ for } \lambda \varepsilon [0,1)\},\ u > 0, \\ \text{and} \\ I(0) := 0, \end{cases}$$

$$(2.2.2) \quad \begin{cases} E(u) := \{x \varepsilon R^n_+ : x \varepsilon L(u),\ y \leq x \text{ imply } y \notin L(u)\},\ u > 0, \\ \text{and} \\ E(0) := 0. \end{cases}$$

It is clear that $E(u) \subset I(u)$ for $u \varepsilon R_+$ but in general, as the following Leontief production structure shows, the converse is not true.

$$(2.2.3) \quad L(u) = \{x \varepsilon R^2_+ : \min\{x_1, x_2\} \geqq u\}.$$

In this example for u = 1, the efficient subset E(1) = (1, 1) while the isoquant I(1) e.g., also contains the point (1, 2).

If the correspondence L is to model a production technology, it must satisfy certain properties (axioms). These are stated in the next definition.

(2.2.4) <u>Definition</u>: A correspondence $L : R_+ \to 2^{R^n_+}$ is called an Input

Correspondence if it satisfies:

L.1 (a) $L(0) = R^n_+$, (b) $0 \notin L(u)$, $u > 0$,

L.2 $\bigcap_{u \in R_+} L(u)$ is empty,

L.3 $x \in L(u)$ implies $\lambda \cdot x \in L(u)$ for $\lambda \geqq 1$,

L.4 (a) $L(u)$ is not empty for some $u > 0$,
(b) if $\lambda \cdot x \in L(u)$ for $u > 0$, the ray $\{\lambda \cdot x : \lambda \geqq 0\}$ intersects all input sets $L(u)$ for $u \in R_+$,

L.5 The correspondence $L: R_+ \rightarrow 2^{R^n_+}$ is closed, i.e., if $(u^\ell \rightarrow u^0, x^\ell \rightarrow x^0$ and $x^\ell \in L(u^\ell)$ for all $\ell)$ then $x^0 \in L(u^0)$,

L.6 $u \geqq v \in R_+$ implies $L(u) \subset L(v)$.

The properties (axioms) L.1-L.6 are referred to here as the weak set of axioms and they are taken as valid for any production technology in a steady state. The first part of L.1 states that null output is obtainable from any input vector in R^n_+, while the second part of L.1 excludes free production, i.e., positive output requires some positive input. However, it does not imply that if each input is applied in a positive amount, output is positive. The implication of property L.2 is that finite amounts of inputs produce finite output. Axiom L.3 models weak disposability of inputs, i.e., increasing inputs with a fixed input mix does not diminish output. Later, strong or free disposability of inputs is defined. Part (a) of property L.4 is included among the axioms in order to avoid a vacuous theory. It guarantees that positive output is obtainable. Part (b) of this axiom relates to attainability of output and states that if positive output is obtainable by some input vector, scaling of the same is possible so that any amount of output can be obtained. L.5 implies that the sets L(u), $u \varepsilon R_+$, are closed, which in turn guarantees that the efficient subsets E(u), $u \varepsilon R_+$, are nonempty (see theorem (2.4.1)). The last property models disposability of output. A weak disposability is taken, since output is a scalar.

In addition to the weak set of axioms, boundedness of the efficient subsets will be assumed to hold in parts of Chapter 3, i.e.,

L.7 E(u) is bounded for $u \varepsilon R_+$.

This axiom, originally proposed by Shephard, is motivated from the physical viewpoint that it can never be efficient to apply unbounded inputs in any production. However, this axiom rules out the Cobb-Douglas production function as well as the CES with elasticities of substitution smaller than one but not zero. Therefore, it will not be assumed to hold in general, but only in the discussion of the laws of bounded output.

Furthermore, strong disposability of inputs and convexity of the input sets L(u) may be imposed on the input structure i.e.,

L.3.S $x \geqq y \varepsilon L(u)$ implies $x \varepsilon L(u)$

and

L.8 L(u) is convex for $u \varepsilon R_+$.

It is clear that if inputs are strongly disposable they are weakly so. However, as the following example illustrates the converse need not hold.

(2.2.5) $L(u) = \{x \varepsilon R^2_+ : \min \{x_1, \max \{0, x_2 - x_1\}\} \geqq u\}$.

The production structure (2.2.5) is homogeneous of degree +1 and therefore satisfies L.3, weak disposability of inputs. However for $(x_1, x_2) = (1, 2) \leq (2, 2) = (y_1, y_2)$, $(x_1, x_2) \varepsilon L(1)$ while $(y_1, y_2) \notin L(1)$. Thus property L.3.S does not apply in this case. See theorems (2.4.8) and (2.4.9) for some implications of strong disposability.

2.3 The Production Function

For an input correspondence $L: R_+ \to 2^{R^n_+}$ satisfying the weak set of axioms, the Production Function is defined as the largest output obtainable from a given input vector. Formally,

$$(2.3.1) \qquad \phi(x) := \max \{u \varepsilon R_+ : x \varepsilon L(u)\}, \; x \varepsilon R^n_+.$$

To show that $\phi: R^n_+ \to R_+$ is well defined let, $x^o \varepsilon R^n_+$. By property L.1, $x^o \varepsilon L(u)$ for some $u \varepsilon R_+$, and by L.2 there is a $u^o \varepsilon R_+$ such that $x^o \notin L(u^o)$. If $\sup\{u \varepsilon R_+ : x^o \varepsilon L(u)\} = u^o = 0$ then $\phi(x^o) = 0$. However, if $u^o > 0$, it follows from L.1 and L.6 that $x^o \varepsilon L(u)$ for all $u \varepsilon [0, u^o)$. Now consider a sequence $\{u^\ell\} \subset [0, u^o)$, with $u^\ell \to u^o$ and $x^\ell \to x^o$ with $x^\ell \varepsilon L(u^o)$ for all ℓ. By property L.5, $x^o \varepsilon L(u^o)$, hence $\max \{u \varepsilon R_+ : x^o \varepsilon L(u)\}$ exists and the production function is well defined.

Before stating the properties of ϕ inherited from those of the input correspondence, consider the upper level set for ϕ, i.e.,

$$(2.3.2) \qquad L_\phi(u) := \{x \varepsilon R^n_+ : \phi(x) \geqq u\}, \; u \varepsilon R_+.$$

The relationship between $L_\phi(u)$ and $L(u)$ is clarified by:

(2.3.3) <u>Theorem</u>: $L_\phi(u) = L(u), \; u \varepsilon R_+$.

Proof: Let $x \varepsilon L_\phi(u)$, $u \varepsilon R_+$, then from the definition of ϕ, see (2.3.1), it follows that $\max \{v \varepsilon R_+ : x \varepsilon L(v)\} \geqq u$, i.e., $x \varepsilon L(u)$ and hence $L_\phi(u) \subset L(u)$. Conversely, let $x \varepsilon L(u)$, then again from (2.3.1) one has $\phi(x) \geqq u$ or $x \varepsilon L_\phi(u)$. Hence $L(u) \subset L_\phi(u)$.

QED.

From theorem (2.3.3) it is clear that $L_\phi(u)$ and $L(u)$ are identical. An immediate corollary to (2.3.1) and (2.3.3) is:

(2.3.4) Corollary: $x \varepsilon L(u)$ if and only if $\phi(x) \geqq u$, $x \varepsilon R^n_+$, $u \varepsilon R_+$.

Using this corollary it is next shown what properties of the production function are equivalent to the properties L.1-L.7 of the input correspondence.

(2.3.5) Theorem: (Shephard, 1967) The production function ϕ satisfies ϕ.1-ϕ.6 if and only if the input correspondence satisfies L.1-L.7.

ϕ.1 (a) $\phi: R^n_+ \to R_+$, (b) $\phi(0) = 0$,

ϕ.2 $\phi(x)$ is bounded for $|| x || < + \infty$,

ϕ.3 $\phi(\lambda \cdot x) \geqq \phi(x)$ for $\lambda \geqq 1$, $x \varepsilon R^n_+$,

ϕ.4 (a) $\phi(x) > 0$ for some $x \varepsilon R^n_+$,
(b) if $\phi(\lambda \cdot x) > 0$, $\phi(\lambda \cdot x) \to + \infty$ as $\lambda \to + \infty$,

ϕ.5 ϕ is upper semi-continuous on R^n_+, i.e., for $x^o \varepsilon R^n_+$, $\lim\sup \phi(x^\ell) \leqq \phi(x^o)$ when $x^\ell \to x^o$,

ϕ.6 $E(u) = \{x \varepsilon R^n_+ : \phi(x) \geqq u,\ y \leq x \text{ imply } \phi(y) < u\}$, $u > 0$, is bounded and $E(0) = 0$.

Proof

(L.1 implies ϕ.1): From (2.3.1) and L.1 first part, it is clear that ϕ

is defined for $x \varepsilon R_+^n$. The second part of $\phi.1$ holds, since if $\phi(0) > 0$, then by corollary (2.3.4), $0 \varepsilon L(u)$, $u > 0$, contradicting L.1 second part.

($\phi.1$ implies L.1): $L(0) = \{x \varepsilon R_+^n : \phi(x) \geqq 0\} = R_+^n$ since $\phi : R_+^n \to R_+$. Next assume $0 \varepsilon L(u)$, $u > 0$, then $\phi(0) = \max \{u \varepsilon R_+ : 0 \varepsilon L(u)\} > 0$ contradicting $\phi.1$ (b).

(L.2 implies $\phi.2$): See (2.3.1) and arguments that follow.

($\phi.2$ implies L.2): Assume $x \varepsilon \bigcap_{u \varepsilon R_+} L(u)$, then $\phi(x) \geqq u$ for each $u \varepsilon R_+$, contradicting $\phi.2$.

(L.3 implies $\phi.3$): For $\lambda \geqq 1$, $x \varepsilon R_+^n$, $\{u \varepsilon R_+ : \lambda \cdot x \varepsilon L(u)\} \supset \{u \varepsilon R_+ : x \varepsilon L(u)\}$ implying that $\phi(\lambda \cdot x) \geqq \phi(x)$.

($\phi.3$ implies L.3): Let $x \varepsilon L(u)$, $u \varepsilon R_+$, then $u \leqq \phi(x) \leqq \phi(\lambda \cdot x)$ for $\lambda \geqq 1$, hence $\lambda \cdot x \varepsilon L(u)$.

(L.4 implies $\phi.4$): (a) $x \varepsilon L(u)$ for some $u > 0$ implies that $\phi(x) \geqq u > 0$, (b) let $\lambda \cdot x \varepsilon L(u)$, $u > 0$ and let $v \varepsilon R_+$. Then by L.4 there is a $\mu > 0$ such that $\mu \cdot x \varepsilon L(v)$ or $\phi(\mu \cdot x) \geqq v$, i.e., $\phi(\mu \cdot x) \to +\infty$ as $\mu \to +\infty$.

($\phi.4$ implies L.4): (a) Let $x \varepsilon R_+^n$ with $\phi(x) \geqq u > 0$, then $x \varepsilon L(u)$, (b) let $\phi(\lambda \cdot x) = u > 0$ and let $v \varepsilon R_+$. Then there is a $\mu > 0$ such that $\phi(\mu \cdot x) \geqq v$, i.e., $\mu \cdot x \varepsilon L(v)$, hence $\{\mu \cdot x : \mu \geqq 0\}$ intersects $L(v)$ for $v \varepsilon R_+$.

(L.5 implies $\phi.5$): Let ($u^\ell = u^o \varepsilon R_+$ for all ℓ, $x^\ell \to x^o$ with $x^\ell \varepsilon L(u^\ell)$ for all ℓ). Then by L.5, $x^o \varepsilon L(u^o)$, i.e., $L(u^o)$ is a closed set. See (6.B.4) for the equivalence between upper semi-continuity and closure of L(u).

(ϕ.5 implies L.5): Let ($u^\ell \to u^o$, $x^\ell \to x^o$ with $x^\ell \varepsilon L(u^\ell)$ for all ℓ). It remains to be shown that $x^o \varepsilon L(u^o)$.

From $x^\ell \varepsilon L(u^\ell)$ it follows that $\phi(x^\ell) \geqq u^\ell$ for all ℓ, see (2.3.4). Therefore, $\limsup_{\ell \to +\infty} \phi(x^\ell) \geqq \limsup_{\ell \to +\infty} u^\ell = u^o$. Since ϕ is upper semi-continuous on R^n_+, $\phi(x^o) \geqq \limsup_{\ell \to +\infty} \phi(x^\ell)$, hence $x^o \varepsilon L(u^o)$.

(L.7 if and only if ϕ.6): Obvious.

Finally, let $u \geqq v \varepsilon R_+$. Then, $L(u) = \{x \varepsilon R^n_+ : \phi(x) \geqq u\} \subset \{x \varepsilon R^n_+ : \phi(x) \geqq v\}$, i.e., property L.6 follows, from the existence of ϕ.

QED.

The properties of the production function equivalent to L.3.S and L.8 of the input correspondence are:

ϕ.3.S $x \geqq y \varepsilon R^n_+$ implies $\phi(x) \geqq \phi(y)$

and

ϕ.8 ϕ is quasi-concave, i.e., $\phi(\lambda \cdot x + (1 - \lambda) \cdot y) \geqq \min\{\phi(x), \phi(y)\}$, $0 \leqq \lambda \leqq 1$, x and $y \varepsilon R^n_+$.

The proof that (L.3.S) holds if and only if (ϕ.3.S), follows like that of (L.3) if and only if (ϕ.3), and is omitted. For the proof of (L.8) equivalent to (ϕ.8), see (6.B.14).

2.4 Properties of the Production Technology

The first property of the technology to be considered is that there is an efficient input vector for each output level.

(2.4.1) Theorem: (Shephard, 1970:a) Let the input correspondence satisfy properties L.1-L.6. E(u) is nonempty, $u \varepsilon R_+$.

Proof: For u = 0, E(0) = 0, therefore let u > 0. Note that by properties L.4, L(u) is nonempty for each u > 0. Define $S_\varepsilon(0) := \{x \varepsilon R^n_+ : \| x \| \leqq \varepsilon\}$ and choose ε so that $L(u) \cap S_\varepsilon(0)$ is nonempty. This intersection is compact since L(u) is closed and $S_\varepsilon(0)$ is compact, see (6.B.2). Therefore, (see (6.B.5)), there is an input vector x^o minimizing the expression $\{\| x \| : x \varepsilon L(u) \cap S_\varepsilon(0)\}$. Now assume $x^o \notin E(u)$. Then there is a $y \varepsilon L(u) \cap S_\varepsilon(0)$, $y \leq x^o$. However, $\| y \| < \| x^o \|$, a contradiction, proves the theorem.

QED.

As pointed out in section 2.2, the property L(u), $u \varepsilon R_+$ closed, is important for the existence of efficient input vectors. The following example shows this.

(2.4.2) $$L(u) := \begin{cases} R^2_+ \text{ for } u = 0 \\ \text{and} \\ \{x \varepsilon R^2_+ : \; x = \lambda \cdot y, \; y = u \cdot [(1-\delta)\cdot(2,2) + \delta \cdot (1,2)], \\ \delta \in [0,1), \; \lambda \geqq 1\}, \text{ for } u > 0. \end{cases}$$

The correspondence given by (2.4.2) satisfies all the weak axioms except L.5. Clearly, the input vector (1,2), which is the only candidate for belonging to E(1), does not belong to L(1). Therefore, E(1) is empty.

It is also of interest to note that the efficient subsets need not be closed. However, since L(u) is closed, $\overline{E(u)} \subset L(u)$. To illustrate the nonclosure of E(u), let the input correspondence be given by:

$$(2.4.3)\quad L(u) := \begin{cases} R_+^2 \text{ for } u = 0 \\ \text{and} \\ \{x \varepsilon R_+^2 : x = \lambda \cdot y,\ \lambda \geqq 1,\ y \varepsilon Z(u)\} \text{ for } u > 0 \end{cases}$$

where $Z(u) := \{y \varepsilon R_+^2 : y = u \cdot [\delta \cdot (2,0) + (1-\delta) \cdot (0,2)],\ \delta \varepsilon [0, \tfrac{1}{4}]\} \cup$
$\{y \varepsilon R_+^2 : y = u \cdot [\gamma \cdot (1,0) + (1-\gamma) \cdot (0,1)],\ \gamma \varepsilon [\tfrac{1}{2}, 1]\}$.

The correspondence (2.4.3) satisfies the weak axioms. For u = 1, $(x_1, x_2) = (0.5, 1.5) \notin E(1)$. However, the sequence $(x_1^\ell, x_2^\ell) := ((4 + 1/\ell)^{-1} \cdot 2,\ (1-(4+1/\ell)^{-1}) \cdot 2) \varepsilon E(1)$ for all $\ell = 1, 2, \ldots$, but $\lim_{\ell \to +\infty} (x_1^\ell, x_2^\ell) = (0.5, 1.5)$. Hence $E(1) \neq \overline{E(1)}$.

A very useful property of the input correspondence is:

(2.4.4) Theorem: (Shephard, 1970:a) Let L satisfy L.1-L.6, $L(u) \subset \overline{E(u)} + R_+^n$, $u \varepsilon R_+$.

Proof: For u = 0, E(0) = 0 and $L(0) = 0 + R_+^n = R_+^n$. Let u > 0 and $x \varepsilon L(u)$ and define $S(x) := \{y \varepsilon R_+^n : y \leqq x\}$. The intersection $L(u) \cap S(x)$ is nonempty and compact, since x belongs to it and S(x) is compact and L(u) is closed. Therefore, (see (6.B.5)).

$$(2.4.5)\quad \min \{ \sum_{i=1}^{n} y_i : y \varepsilon L(u) \cap S(x)\}$$

exists. Let y^0 be a vector minimizing (2.4.5). Then $y^0 \varepsilon \overline{E(u)}$, otherwise there would be a $z \varepsilon L(u) \cap S(x)$, $z \leq y$ contradicting the property of y^o. Also, $x = y^o + (x-y^o)$ where $(x-y^o)\varepsilon R^n_+$. Consequently, $L(u) \subset \overline{E(u)} + R^n_+$.

QED.

If in addition to the weak axioms, the production structure obeys strong disposability of inputs, the following holds true:

(2.4.6) <u>Theorem</u>: (Shephard, 1970:a) If L.3.S applies in addition to L.1-L.6, $L(u) = \overline{E(u)} + R^n_+$, $u\varepsilon R_+$.

Proof: One need only prove that for $u > 0$, $\overline{E(u)} + R^n_+ \subset L(u)$. Let $x\varepsilon\overline{E(u)} \subset L(u)$ then for $y\varepsilon R^n_+$, $(x + y) \geqq x$ and hence by L.3.S, $(x + y)\varepsilon L(u)$.

QED.

An implication of strong disposability of inputs, of interest in the discussion of null jointness among inputs, is next derived. But first introduce:

(2.4.7) $C(u) := \{x\varepsilon R^n_+ : x = \lambda \cdot y,\ \lambda > 0,\ y\varepsilon L(u)\}$, $u > 0$,

the cone spanned by the input set $L(u)$ for $u > 0$. Note that by property L.4(a), $C(u)$ is nonempty and by L.4(b), $C(u) = C(1)$ for all $u > 0$.

(2.4.8) <u>Theorem</u>: (Färe and Jansson, 1974:a) Let the input correspondence satisfy L.1-L.6 and L.3.S. Then $\overline{C(1)} = R^n_+$.

This theorem states that if inputs are strictly positive i.e., $x > 0$, then for all $u > 0$ there exists a $\lambda > 0$ such that $\lambda \cdot x\varepsilon L(u)$.

Proof of theorem (2.4.8): Clearly, $\overline{C(1)} \subset R^n_+$, therefore assume that

$x \varepsilon \overset{\circ}{R}{}^n_+$. By property L.4(a), there is an input vector $y \varepsilon L(u)$ for some $u > 0$ and by strong disposability there is a $z \varepsilon L(u)$, $z \geqq y$ such that $x = \lambda \cdot z$ for some $\lambda \geqq 0$, proving the theorem.

QED.

If it is assumed that L(u) is convex, $u \varepsilon R_+$, one can prove:

(2.4.9) Theorem: (Färe and Jansson, 1975) Let the input correspondence satisfy L.1-L.6 and L.8. Then it will exhibit strong disposability of inputs if and only if $\overline{C(1)} = R^n_+$.

Proof: Since theorem (2.4.8) holds, it is sufficient (given L.1-L.6 and L.8) to prove that $\overline{C(1)} = R^n_+$ implies strong disposability of inputs. Let $x \geqq y \varepsilon L(u)$, $u > 0$. If $x = y$ then $x \varepsilon L(u)$, thus let $x \geq y$ and assume $x \notin L(u)$. The input set L(u) is convex, property L.8, it is closed, property L.5. Thus, by the separation theorem, see (6.B.16), there is a hyperplane H such that L(u) is contained in the closed (upper) halfspace H^+ generated by H. Since $x \notin H^+$ and $x \geq y$, the hyperplane H is not parallel to any subspace of dimension (n-1) with a component $z_i = 0$ of $z = (z_1, \ldots, z_i \ldots, z_n) \varepsilon R^n_+$. Thus there are three possibilities: (a) H separates L(u) and 0, (b) H goes through 0 or (c) H does not separate L(u) and 0. In the first two cases there are, due to the nonparallelity of H, elements of R^n_+ not belonging to $\overline{C(1)}$. In case (c), when H does not separate L(u) and 0, $\overline{C(1)} \subset H^+$ due to property L.3. Thus, if $x \notin L(u)$, $\overline{C(1)} \neq R^n_+$, contradicting the hypothesis. Therefore, $x \varepsilon L(u)$, proving the theorem.

QED.

The following figure shows a counter example to theorem (2.4.9) when L(u), $u \varepsilon R_+$, is not convex.

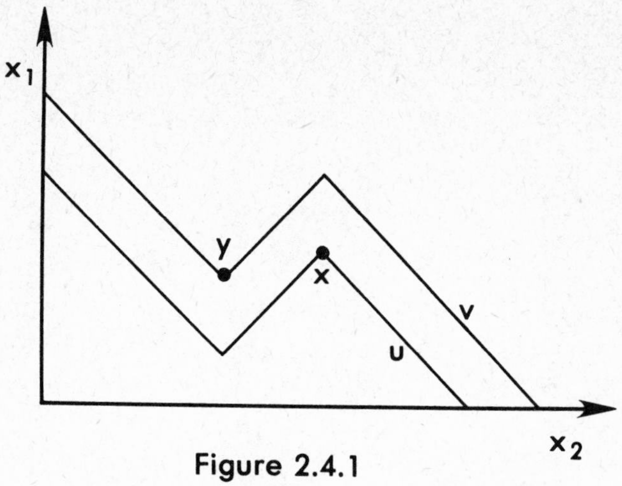

Figure 2.4.1

In this figure, $x\varepsilon L(u)$ and $y\varepsilon L(v)$, with $v > u$. Also, $x \geq y$, but $x \notin L(v)$.

As pointed out in section 2.2, in general, the efficient subset $E(u)$ and the isoquant $I(u)$, $u > 0$, do not coincide, but $E(u)$ is a proper subset of $I(u)$, $u > 0$. It is of some interest to show sufficient conditions for $E(u) = I(u)$.

(2.4.10) Theorem: If the production function ϕ is continuous on R^n_+ and satisfies $\phi.1$-$\phi.5$, and if $x \geq y$ implies $\phi(x) > \phi(u)$, then $E(u) = I(u)$, $u\varepsilon R_+$.

Proof: It is first shown that continuity of ϕ implies $I(u) \subset \{x\varepsilon R^n_+ : \phi(x) = u\}$. Clearly, $I(u) \subset L(u) := \{x\varepsilon R^n_+ : \phi(x) \geqq u\}$. Hence assume $x^o \varepsilon \{x\varepsilon R^n_+ : \phi(x) > u\}$. Since ϕ is continuous, the set $\{x\varepsilon R^n_+ : \phi(x) > u\}$ is open (see (6.B.7)) implying that there is a neighborhood of x^o contained in this set. Thus, $x^o \notin I(u)$. Therefore, ϕ continuous implies $I(u) \subset \{x\varepsilon R^n_+ : \phi(x) = u\}$, $u\varepsilon R_+$. Since by definition $E(0) = I(0)$, let $\overline{u} > 0$. By $\phi.4$ and continuity there is an input vector $\overline{x}\varepsilon R^n_+$ such that $\phi(\overline{x}) = \overline{u}$. Now assume that $x \notin E(\phi(\overline{x}))$. If $x \notin L(\phi(\overline{x}))$, $x \notin I(\phi(\overline{x}))$ so let $x\varepsilon L(\phi(\overline{x}))$. There is then a $y\varepsilon L(\phi(\overline{x}))$, $y \leq x$, implying that $\phi(x) > \phi(y)$

by the condition stated in the theorem. Also, since $y \varepsilon L(\phi(\bar{x}))$, $\phi(x) > \phi(y) \geqq \phi(\bar{x})$ and hence $\phi(x) > \phi(\bar{x})$. Since $I(u) \subset \{x \varepsilon R_+^n: \phi(x) = u\}$, $x \notin I(\phi(\bar{x}))$. Hence $I(u) \subset E(u) \subset I(u)$.

QED.

Two corollaries follow from this theorem, first:

(2.4.11) Corollary: If the production function ϕ satisfies the conditions of theorem (2.4.10), then $I(u) := \{x \varepsilon R_+^n: \phi(x) = u\}$.

Proof: In the proof of theorem (2.4.10) it was shown that $I(u) \subset \{x \varepsilon R_+^n: \phi(x) = u\}$, $u \varepsilon R_+$. Clearly, $I(0) = \{x \varepsilon R_+^n: \phi(x) = 0\}$ by the property; $x \geq y$ implies $\phi(x) > \phi(y)$. Furthermore, assume $x \notin I(u)$, $u > 0$, then by the same property, $\phi(x)$ is either strictly less or strictly greater than u, implying that $x \notin \{x \varepsilon R_+^n: \phi(x) = u\}$.

QED.

This corollary states sufficient conditions, justifying a common practice of defining the isoquant $I(u)$ by $\{x \varepsilon R_+^n: \phi(x) = u\}$, $u \varepsilon R_+$.

(2.4.12) Corollary: If the production function satisfies the conditions of theorem (2.4.10), then $\overline{E(u)} = E(u) = I(u) = \overline{I(u)}$, $u \varepsilon R_+$. If also ϕ.6 applies, then these sets are compact.

Proof: By corollary (2.4.11), $I(u) = \{x \varepsilon R_+^n: \phi(x) = u\}$, $u \varepsilon R_+$. Since ϕ is assumed to be continuous, the sets $L(u) := \{x \varepsilon R_+^n: \phi(x) \geqq u\}$ and $\ell(u) := \{x \varepsilon R_+^n: \phi(x) \leqq u\}$ are closed, by (6.B.7). Hence $I(u) = L(u) \cap \ell(u)$ is closed. Thus by theorem (2.4.10) the first part is proved. The second part holds since a closed and bounded subset of R_+^n with its natural topology is compact.

QED.

2.5 Special Production Structures

In this section some special production structures, useful for this monograph, are introduced. This section is not intended to be a complete catalog of special structures, but a sample of some important examples.

Following Shephard (1953) and (1970:a) the Distance Function ψ for an input set $L(u)$, $u \varepsilon R_+$ is defined as:

$$(2.5.1) \quad \psi(u, x) := [\min \{\lambda \varepsilon R_+ : \lambda \cdot x \varepsilon L(u)\}]^{-1}$$

Note that $\psi(u, \lambda \cdot x) = \lambda \cdot \psi(u, x)$, $\lambda > 0$ and that $L(u) = \{x \varepsilon R_+^n : \psi(u, x) \geqq 1\}$.

Again following Shephard (1953) and (1970:a), a production function is Homothetic if:

$$(2.5.2) \quad \phi(x) := F(\psi(1, x))$$

where $F: R_+ \to R_+$ has the properties: $F(0) = 0$, $F(v)$ is finite for $|| v || < +\infty$, F is nondecreasing, $F(v) \to +\infty$ as $v \to +\infty$ and F is upper semi-continuous. ψ is the distance function for $L(1)$.

The properties of F allow the following definitions of the inverses of F and F^{-1}:

$$(2.5.3) \quad \begin{cases} F^{-1}(u) := \min \{v : F(v) \geqq u\}, \ u \varepsilon R_+ \\ \text{and} \\ F(v) := \max \{u : F^{-1}(u) \leqq v\}, \ v \varepsilon R_+ \end{cases}$$

One can prove the following property for a homothetic

production structure.

(2.5.4) Theorem: $\phi(x) = F(\psi(1,x))$ if and only if $L(u) = F^{-1}(u)\cdot L(1)$.

Proof: Let $\phi(x) = F(\psi(1,x))$ and consider

$$
\begin{aligned}
(2.5.5) \quad L(u) &= \{x\varepsilon R^n_+ : F(\psi(1,x)) \geqq u\} && \text{(corollary 2.3.4)}\\
&= \{x\varepsilon R^n_+ : \psi(1,x) \geqq F^{-1}(u)\} && \text{(definition 2.5.3)}\\
&= F^{-1}(u)\cdot L(1) && \text{(property of } \psi(1,x)).
\end{aligned}
$$

Conversely:

$$
\begin{aligned}
(2.5.6) \quad \phi(x) :&= \max\{u : x\varepsilon F^{-1}(u)\cdot L(1)\}\\
&= \max\{u : \psi(1,x)\cdot(F^{-1}(u))^{-1} \geqq 1\}\\
&= F(\psi(1,x)).
\end{aligned}
$$

QED.

For other properties of the homothetic production function see Färe (1973), Färe and Shephard (1977).

The following generalizations of homogeneous and homothetic into almost homogeneous and almost homothetic production structures are important for the discussion of the law of diminishing returns at the extensive margin.

A production function $\Omega : R^n_+ \to R_+$ is called Almost Homogeneous if for all $\lambda > 0$

$$
(2.5.7) \quad \Omega(\lambda^{\alpha_1}\cdot x_1, \lambda^{\alpha_2}\cdot x_2, \ldots, \lambda^{\alpha_n}\cdot x_n) = \lambda\cdot\Omega(x_1, x_2, \ldots, x_n)
$$

where $\alpha_i > 0$, $(i = 1,2,\ldots, n)$, are fixed numbers. See Aczél (1966) for the concept of almost homogeneity. A production function is called Almost Homothetic if

$$(2.5.8) \quad \phi(x) = F(\Omega(x))$$

where Ω is almost homogeneous, with properties compatible with the production axioms and where F has the properties of (2.5.2).

The following two-factor Weak Disposability of Inputs (WDI) production function is used frequently in this monograph. It is an example of a production structure satisfying the weak axioms with bounded efficient subsets.

$$(2.5.9) \quad \phi(x_1, x_2) := \begin{cases} A\cdot[\delta\cdot(x_1-\beta_2\cdot x_2)^{-\rho} + (1-\delta)\cdot(x_2-\beta_1\cdot x_1)^{-\rho}]^{-1/\rho} \\ \text{if } (x_i-\beta_j\cdot x_j) \geqq 0,\ i\neq j,\ i,j=1,2. \\ 0 \text{ otherwise.} \end{cases}$$

where $A > 0$, $\delta\varepsilon(0,1)$, $\rho\varepsilon(-1, +\infty)$ and $\beta_j\varepsilon[0, +\infty)$ with $(\beta_2)^{-1} > \beta_1$ for $\beta_2 > 0$.

For any value of the parameters, $\phi(0,0) = 0$ and $\phi(x_1, x_2)$ is bounded for $||(x_1, x_2)|| < +\infty$. The WDI function is homogeneous of degree +1, therefore it satisfies properties ϕ.3 and ϕ.4(b). For $(x_i-\beta_j\ x_j) > 0$, $i\neq j$, $i,j=1,2$, the function is strictly positive and hence satisfies ϕ.4(a). It is clearly upper semi-continuous. Finally for $\beta_1, \beta_2 > 0$ and the condition $(\beta_2)^{-1} > \beta_1$, the set $\{x\varepsilon R^2_+ : \phi(x_1,x_2) > 0\}$ is a cone such that if (x_1,x_2) belongs to this cone, $x_i > 0$, $i=1,2$. Therefore, the efficient subsets $E(u)$, $u > 0$, are bounded. Thus, the WDI production function is an example of a production technology satisfying the weak set of axioms. One also notes that the function is quasi-concave, but for $\beta_i > 0$, i=1,2, $(\beta_2)^{-1} > \beta_1$, it does not obey strong disposability of inputs. For other properties of this production function see Färe and Jansson (1975).

It is noteworthy that for $\beta_i = 0$, i=1,2, the WDI function degenerates into the CES. Therefore, among others, it contains the Cobb-Douglas and (a form of) Leontief production functions as special cases. The three functions are:

(2.5.10) $\phi(x_1, x_2) := A \cdot [\delta \cdot x_1^{-\rho} + (1 \cdot \delta) x_2^{-\rho}]^{-1/\rho}$

(2.5.11) $\phi(x_1, x_2) := A \cdot x_1^{\delta} \cdot x_2^{(1-\delta)}$

(2.5.12) $\phi(x_1, x_2) := A \cdot \min \{x_1, x_2\}$,

respectively.

3. LAWS OF BOUNDED OUTPUT AND DIMINISHING AVERAGE RETURNS

3.1 Introduction

A fundamental methodological question in the economic theory of production is whether or not a positive bound on a certain subset of factors bounds output. Frequently, when a distinction is drawn between stock and flow inputs, one addresses oneself to this question in terms of capacity. Capacity is understood to mean the largest possible output obtainable given fixed stock and variable flow inputs. Rather than distinguishing between stock and flow, in this chapter we will apply the notion of an essential subset of factors of production, or equivalently, an essential factor combination. A factor combination is essential if, when it is not used in production, output is zero.

In section 3.2, it is shown that a factor combination is essential if and only if there is a positive bound on those factors such that output is bounded, yet the other factors are allowed to vary freely. That is a factor combination is essential if and only if it is weak limitational. This basic equivalence was first shown by Shephard (see Shephard, 1970: a,b). Shephard assumes that the production technology satisfies axioms ϕ.1-ϕ.6, ϕ.3.S and ϕ.8. Here an alternative proof is given involving only ϕ.1-ϕ.6. The axiom ϕ.6 rules out the CES functions with positive elasticity of substitution equal to or smaller than one. These functions are frequently applied in economics, therefore, it is desirable to formulate a weaker condition so that a factor combination is essential if and only if it is weak limitational. Such a sufficient condition is introduced in section 3.2.

A factor combination is called strong limitational if each positive bound on it bounds output. In section 3.3 strong limitationality is discussed. Conditions on the production structure are derived for a factor combination to be weak limitational if and only if it is strong limitational, and for a factor combination to be essential if and only if it is strong limitational.

The necessity of the production axioms for output to be bounded is discussed in section 3.4. By counterexamples minimal subsets are established.

A law of bounded average returns is discussed in section 3.5. First, conditions on subsets of production factors are stated sufficient for the law to apply. Then, using functional equations, a characterization of the production structure is derived which is necessary and sufficient for the law of bounded average returns to hold.

3.2 Essential and Weak Limitational Subsets of Factors of Production

A production technology may be such that it is necessary that certain inputs are used in production to obtain positive output. In this case, one relates to an essential subset of production factors or an essential factor combination.

Denote by

(3.2.1) $$D(\nu_1,\nu_2,\ldots,\nu_k) := \{x \varepsilon R^n_+ : \ x \geq 0,\ x_{\nu_i} = 0,\ i = 1,2,\ldots,k\}$$ [1)]

the subcone of R^n_+ spanned by x_{ν_j}, $j = k + 1, k + 2,\ldots,n$, not containing the vertex. Then formally:

(3.2.2) Definition: (Shephard, 1970: a,b) A factor combination $\{\nu_1,\nu_2,\ldots,\nu_k\}$, $(1 \leqq k < n)$, is Essential (for the production of output u) if $\phi(x) = 0$ for $x \varepsilon D(\nu_1,\nu_2,\ldots,\nu_k)$ or equivalently, $L(u) \cap D(\nu_1,\nu_2,\ldots,\nu_k)$ empty for $u > 0$.

Note that k in this definition and in those to follow, is restricted to $k < n$. This is done to avoid a trivial case, see ϕ.1. To elucidate the notion of essentiality, let a two-input, one-output technology be modelled by a WDI production function, namely:

(3.2.3) $$\phi(x_1,x_2) := \begin{cases} A\cdot[(1-\delta)\cdot(x_1-\beta_2\cdot x_2)^{-\rho} + \delta\cdot x_2^{-\rho}]^{-1/\rho} \\ \text{if } (x_1-\beta_2\cdot x_2) \geqq 0 \\ 0 \text{ otherwise} \end{cases}$$

with the parameters restricted as: $A > 0$, $\delta\varepsilon(0,1)$, $\rho\varepsilon(-1,0)$ and $\beta_2\varepsilon(0, +\infty)$. If the second factor in example (3.2.3) is zero, output

---

1) $\overline{D}(\nu_1,\nu_2,\ldots,\nu_k) := D(\nu_1,\nu_2,\ldots,\nu_k) \cup \{0\}$.

is possible by applying the first factor in any positive amount, therefore x_2 is not essential. However, if $x_1 = 0$, then no output can be produced using only x_2, i.e., the first factor is essential.

It is clear from Definition (3.2.2) that if a factor combination $\{\nu_1, \nu_2, \ldots, \nu_k\}$ is essential, any combination containing that subset is also essential. The converse, however, may or may not be true. One therefore defines:

(3.2.4) Definition: (Färe, 1972) An essential factor combination $\{\nu_1, \nu_2, \ldots, \nu_k\}$, $(1 \leqq k < n)$, is Irreducible if and only if any proper subset of $\{\nu_1, \nu_2, \ldots, \nu_k\}$ is not essential.

Let a three-input one-output technology be given by

$$(3.2.5) \quad \phi(x_1, x_2, x_3) := \begin{cases} A \cdot [(1-\delta) \cdot (x_1 + x_2 - \beta_3 \cdot x_3)^{-\rho} + \delta \cdot x_3^{-\rho}]^{-1/\rho} \\ \text{if } (x_1 + x_2 - \beta_3 \cdot x_3) \geqq 0 \\ 0 \text{ otherwise} \end{cases}$$

where the parameters are restricted as follows: $A > 0$, $\delta \varepsilon (0,1)$, $\rho \varepsilon (-1,0)$ and $\beta_3 \varepsilon (0, +\infty)$. Clearly, x_3 is not an essential factor, nor are the two factor combinations $\{x_1\}$ or $\{x_2\}$. However, the combination $\{x_1, x_2\}$ is, showing an example of an irreducible essential factor combination.

Attention is now turned to the second important concept discussed in this section, namely weak limitationality.

(3.2.6) Definition: (Shephard, 1970: a,b) A factor combination $\{\nu_1, \nu_2, \ldots, \nu_k\}$, $(1 \leqq k < n)$, is Weak Limitational (for the production of output u), if there exists a positive bound, B, such that output $\phi(x)$ is bounded for all $x\varepsilon\{x\varepsilon R^n_+: || x_{\nu_1}, x_{\nu_2},\ldots,x_{\nu_k} || \leqq B\}$.

This definition requires only that there exist one positive bound on the subvector $(x_{\nu_1},x_{\nu_2},\ldots,x_{\nu_k})$ which bounds output. This does not imply that output should be bounded for each such bound. (This issue is discussed in the next section.) Nor is it required that output be positive for the bound on $(x_{\nu_1},x_{\nu_2},\ldots,x_{\nu_k})$. The following is an example of a technology which illustrates weak limitationality.

$$(3.2.7) \quad \phi(x_1,x_2) := \begin{cases} A\cdot[(1-\delta)\cdot x_1^{-\rho} + \delta\cdot(x_2-\beta)^{-\rho}]^{-1/\rho} \\ \text{if } (x_2-\beta) \geqq 0 \\ 0 \text{ otherwise} \end{cases}$$

where $A,\ \beta > 0$, $\delta\varepsilon(0,1)$ and $\rho\varepsilon(-1,0)$. It is clear that the second factor is weak limitational, since for a positive bound $x_2^0\varepsilon(0,\beta)$, output is zero and therefore bounded.

To establish the next theorem the following lemma is useful.

(3.2.8) <u>Lemma</u>: For $u > 0$, $D(\nu_1,\nu_2,..,\nu_k) \cap L(u)$, $(1\leqq k<n)$, is empty if and only if $D(\nu_1,\nu_2,\ldots,\nu_k) \cap \overline{E(u)}$ is empty.

Proof: Let $D(\nu_1,\nu_2,\ldots,\nu_k) \cap L(u)$ be empty, then since $\overline{E(u)} \subset L(u)$, so is $D(\nu_1,\nu_2,\ldots,\nu_k) \cap \overline{E(u)}$. If $D(\nu_1,\nu_2,\ldots,\nu_k) \cap \overline{E(u)}$ is empty, $\overline{E(u)} \subset (R^n_+ \setminus D(\nu_1,\nu_2,\ldots,\nu_k))$ and $(\overline{E(u)} + R^n_+) \subset (R^n_+ \setminus D(\nu_1,\nu_2,\ldots,\nu_k))$. Therefore, since $L(u) \subset (\overline{E(u)} + R^n_+)$, (see 2.4.4), $D(\nu_1,\nu_2,\ldots,\nu_k) \cap L(u)$ is empty.

QED.

An important theorem is proved next. It was originally (under stronger assumptions on the technology) shown by Shephard (see Shephard, 1970:a and 1970:b). The theorem establishes the equivalence between essentiality and weak limitationality of a factor combination. The proof given here invokes only $\phi.1$-$\phi.6$, and it differs in structure from that of Shephard.

(3.2.9) Theorem: For a production technology satisfying the axioms $\phi.1$-$\phi.6$, or equivalently L.1-L.7, a factor combination $\{\nu_1,\nu_2,\ldots,\nu_k\}$, $(1\leq k<n)$, is weak limitational if and only if it is essential.

Proof: Assume first that the factor combination is not essential. Then there is an input vector $x^o \varepsilon D(\nu_1,\nu_2,\ldots,\nu_k)$ such that $\phi(x^o) > 0$. Hence by property $\phi.4$(b), that factor combination is not weak limitational, proving the first part of the theorem.

To prove the converse, assume that $\{\nu_1,\nu_2,\ldots,\nu_k\}$ is an essential factor combination. Then for any positive output rate u, $D(\nu_1,\nu_2,\ldots,\nu_k) \cap \overline{E(u)}$ is empty by lemma (3.2.8). Define $\overline{D}(\nu_1,\nu_2,\ldots,\nu_k) := (D(\nu_1,\nu_2,\ldots,\nu_k) \cup \{0\})$. This set is closed and for $u > 0$ its intersection with $\overline{E(u)}$ is empty. Let $x \varepsilon \overline{E(u)}$, $u > 0$, then $\overline{E(u)}$ is nonempty since L(u) is nonempty (see (2.4.1)). L(u) nonempty follows from property $\phi.4$. Therefore it follows that the distance

$$(3.2.10) \quad d(x,\overline{D}(\nu_1,\nu_2,\ldots,\nu_k)) := \inf\{\|x-y\| : y \varepsilon \overline{D}(\nu_1,\nu_2,\ldots,\nu_k)\}$$

is strictly positive, see (6.B.11). The function (3.2.10) is continuous in x (see (6.B.12)), and since $\overline{E(u)}$ is a compact set there is an input vector $x^o \varepsilon \overline{E(u)}$ such that x^o minimizes (see (6.B.5)) the expression

(3.2.11) $0 < \delta := \min \{d(x,\bar{D}(\nu_1,\nu_2,\ldots,\nu_k)) : x\varepsilon\overline{E(u)}\}$.

Choose as the positive bound $B = \delta/2$. By theorem (2.4.4), $L(u) \subset (\overline{E(u)} + R^n_+)$. It follows from properties L.6 of the input correspondence that the intersection $(L(v) \cap \{x\varepsilon R^n_+ : \| x_{\nu_1}, x_{\nu_2}, \ldots, x_{\nu_k} \| \leqq B\})$ is empty for all $v \geqq u$, i.e., $\phi(x)$ is bounded for $x\varepsilon\{x\varepsilon R^n_+ : \| x_{\nu_1}, x_{\nu_2}, \ldots, x_{\nu_k} \| \leqq B\}$.

QED.

From this proof it is clear that the assumption of bounded efficient subsets (ϕ.6) can be relaxed to prove theorem (3.2.9). Therefore, consider the function

(3.2.12) $f(u/\nu_1,\nu_2,\ldots,\nu_k) := \inf \{d(x,y) : x\varepsilon\overline{E(u)},\ y\varepsilon\bar{D}(\nu_1,\nu_2,\ldots,\nu_k)\}$

where $d(x,y)$ is the Euclidean distance between x and y. First note:

(3.2.13) <u>Lemma</u>: Let the production function satisfy ϕ.1-ϕ.5. A factor combination $\{\nu_1,\nu_2,\ldots,\nu_k\}$, $(1 \leqq k < n)$, is not essential if and only if $f(u/\nu_1,\nu_2,\ldots,\nu_k) = 0$ for all $u > 0$, and the infinum in (3.2.12) is a minimum.

The proof is immediate, but note that from axioms ϕ.4(b) it follows that if $f(u/\nu_1,\nu_2,\ldots,\nu_k) = 0$ for some $u > 0$ and the infinum is a minimum, then $f(u/\nu_1,\nu_2,\ldots,\nu_k) = 0$ for all $u > 0$. The function (3.2.12) is related to essentiality by:

(3.2.14) <u>Corollary</u>: Let ϕ satisfy ϕ.1-ϕ.5. If a factor combination $\{\nu_1,\nu_2,\ldots,\nu_k\}$ is essential, then either (i) if $f(u/\nu_1,\nu_2,\ldots,\nu_k) = 0$ for some $u > 0$, the infinum in (3.2.12) is not a minimum or (ii) if $f(u/\nu_1,\nu_2,\ldots,\nu_k) > 0$ for all $u > 0$, the infinum may or may not be a minimum.

This corollary follows from lemma (3.2.13). Note that if it is assumed that the efficient subsets are bounded, then in (i) the infinum is a minimum, and hence by lemma (3.2.13), $\{\nu_1,\nu_2,\ldots,\nu_k\}$ is not essential. The following remark clarifies the next theorem.

(3.2.15) Remark: A factor combination $\{\nu_1,\nu_2,\ldots,\nu_k\}$, $(1 \leqq k < n)$, is weak limitational if and only if $f(u/\nu_1,\nu_2,\ldots,\nu_k) > 0$ for some $u > 0$.

Proof: If $\{\nu_1,\nu_2,\ldots,\nu_k\}$ is weak limitational, then there exists a positive bound B such that $\sup\{\phi(x)\colon x \varepsilon R^n_+, \| x_{\nu_1},x_{\nu_2},\ldots,x_{\nu_k} \| \leqq B\} = u^o < +\infty$. Therefore, the intersection $L(u) \cap \{x\varepsilon R^n_+\colon \| x_{\nu_1},x_{\nu_2},\ldots, x_{\nu_k} \| \leqq B/2\}$ is empty for all $u \geqq u^o$. Hence, $f(u/\nu_1,\nu_2,\ldots,\nu_k) \geqq B/2 > 0$ for all $u \geqq u^o$. Conversely, assume $f(u^o/\nu_1,\nu_2,\ldots,\nu_k) > 0$ for $u^o > 0$. Then the intersection $\overline{E(u)} \cap \{x\varepsilon R^n_+\colon \| x_{\nu_1},x_{\nu_2},\ldots,x_{\nu_k} \| \leqq f(u^o/\nu_1,\nu_2,\ldots,\nu_k)/2\}$ is empty for all $u \geqq u^o$. The remark now follows from theorem (2.4.4).

QED.

Therefore:

(3.2.16) Theorem: Let the production function satisfy properties $\phi.1$-$\phi.5$. Let the factor combination $\{\nu_1,\nu_2,\ldots,\nu_k\}$, $(1 \leqq k < n)$, be essential and assume that the technology satisfies (*): if $f(u/\nu_1,\nu_2,\ldots,\nu_k) = 0$ there is an $x\varepsilon\overline{E(u)}$ and a $y\varepsilon\overline{D}(\nu_1,\nu_2,\ldots,\nu_k)$ such that $f(u/\nu_1,\nu_2,\ldots,\nu_k) = 0$, $(x = y)$. Then, $\{\nu_1,\nu_2,\ldots,\nu_k\}$ is weak limitational.

The economic meaning of the (*) condition is straightforward. It asserts that at each positive output level complete substitution of $(x_{\nu_1}, x_{\nu_2}, \ldots, x_{\nu_k})$ by any subset of factors in $\{\nu_{k+1}, \nu_{k+2}, \ldots, \nu_n\}$ with its norm unbounded is not possible. Note that the Cobb-Douglas production function (2.5.11) does not satisfy the (*) condition, but the other CES functions do. In addition, the affinely homogeneous Cobb-Douglas production function satisfies the (*) condition. (For a discussion of affinely homogeneous production functions, see Färe and Lovell, 1979). Consider,

$$(3.2.17) \qquad \phi(x_1, x_2) := (\max\{0, x_1 - a_1\})^{\alpha} \cdot (\max\{0, x_2 - a_2\})^{1-\alpha}$$

where $a_i > 0$, $(i = 1,2)$ and $0 < \alpha < 1$. This affinely homogeneous Cobb-Douglas production function satisfies the conditions of theorem (3.2.16) but it has not bounded efficient subsets. However, the first factor is both essential and weak limitational, therefore theorem (3.2.16) generalizes theorem (3.2.9).

It is of interest to know that weak limitationality does not imply the (*) condition. To see this, consider the following production function

$$(3.2.18) \qquad \phi(x_1, x_2) := \begin{cases} x_1 \cdot x_2 \text{ for } x \varepsilon \underline{\overline{X}} \\ 1 \text{ for } x \varepsilon (R_+^2 \setminus \{\underline{\overline{X}} \cup \underline{\overline{Y}}\}) \\ \min\{x_1, x_2\} \text{ for } x \varepsilon \underline{\overline{Y}} \end{cases}$$

where $\underline{\overline{X}} := \{x \varepsilon R_+^2 : x_1 \cdot x_2 \leqq 1\}$ and $\underline{\overline{Y}} := \{x \varepsilon R_+^2 : x_i > 1,\ i = 1,2\}$. This production function satisfies properties $\phi.1$-$\phi.5$, it has unbounded efficient subsets for $u \varepsilon (0,1)$ and bounded elsewhere. The first factor is clearly weak limitational, and $f(u/1) = 0$ for $u \varepsilon (0,1)$, but there is no $x \varepsilon \overline{E(u)}$ and no $y \varepsilon D(S)$ such that $f(u/1) = d(x,y) = 0$.

3.3 Essential and Strong Limitational Subsets of Factors of Production

For a factor combination to be weak limitational it is required only that there be one positive bound on these factors that bounds output. Example (3.2.7) shows a case in which positive bounds on the essential factor result in either zero (and bounded) output or in output which tends to infinity when the non-essential factor tends to infinity. To eliminate such technologies, define:

(3.3.1) Definition: (Shephard, 1970: a,b) A factor combination $\{\nu_1,\nu_2,\ldots,\nu_k\}$, $(1 \leqq k<n)$, is Strong Limitational if for each positive bound B, $\phi(x)$ is bounded for $x \varepsilon \{x \varepsilon R^n_+ : \| x_{\nu_1}, x_{\nu_2}, \ldots, x_{\nu_k} \| \leqq B\}$.

Consider again the function:

$$(3.2.12) \quad f(u/\nu_1,\nu_2,\ldots,\nu_k) = \inf\{d(x,y) : x \varepsilon \overline{E(u)},\ y \varepsilon \overline{D}(\nu_1,\nu_2,\ldots,\nu_k)\}.$$

In terms of this function one has the following characterization of strong limitationality.

(3.3.2) Theorem: Let the production structure satisfy $\phi.1$-$\phi.5$ or equivalently L.1-L.6. A factor combination $\{\nu_1,\nu_2,\ldots,\nu_k\}$, $(1 \leqq k<n)$, is strong limitational if and only if (**) $f(u/\nu_1,\nu_2,\ldots,\nu_k) \to +\infty$ as $u \to +\infty$.

Proof: First assume that (**) does not hold. Then, there is a positive real number C such that $f(u/\nu_1,\nu_2,\ldots,\nu_k) \leqq C$ for all $u > 0$. Choose a positive bound B on $(x_{\nu_1}, x_{\nu_2}, \ldots, x_{\nu_k})$ such that $B > C$. Then the intersection $(L(u) \cap \{x \varepsilon R^n_+ : \| x_{\nu_1}, x_{\nu_2}, \ldots, x_{\nu_k} \| \leqq B\})$ is nonempty for all $u > 0$, contradicting strong limitationality of $\{\nu_1,\nu_2,\ldots,\nu_k\}$.

Conversely, assume that (**) holds. Let B be an arbitrary bound on $(x_{\nu_1}, x_{\nu_2}, \ldots, x_{\nu_k})$. Then by (**) there is a u(B) such that the intersection $(\overline{E(u)} \cap \{x \varepsilon R^n_+ : \| x_{\nu_1}, x_{\nu_2}, \ldots, x_{\nu_k} \} \| \leq B\})$ is empty for all $u \geq u(B)$. Hence by theorem (2.4.4), $\phi(x)$ is bounded for all $x \varepsilon \{x \varepsilon R^n_+ : \| x_{\nu_1}, x_{\nu_2}, \ldots, x_{\nu_k} \| \leq B\}$.

QED.

Clearly, if a factor combination is strong limitational it is weak limitational. However, as example (3.2.7) shows, the converse is not true, not even when the production structure has bounded efficient subsets.

It is of interest to note that for a homothetic production structure a factor combination is weak limitational if and only if it is strong limitational.

(3.3.3) <u>Theorem</u>: Assume the production structure is homothetic and satisfies $\phi.1$-$\phi.5$. A factor combination $\{\nu_1, \nu_2, \ldots, \nu_k\}$, $(1 \leq k < n)$, is weak limitational if and only if it is strong limitational.

Proof: It is sufficient to prove that weak limitationality implies strong limitationality. The production structure is assumed to be homothetic, thus by theorems (2.5.4) and (2.4.4), $L(u) \subset F^{-1}(u) \cdot (\overline{E(1)} + R^n_+)$. Since $\{\nu_1, \nu_2, \ldots, \nu_k\}$ is weak limitational, by remark (3.2.15), $f(1/\nu_1, \nu_2, \ldots, \nu_k) > 0$. Thus, $F^{-1}(u) \to +\infty$ as $u \to +\infty$ implies that $f(u/\nu_1, \nu_2, \ldots, \nu_k) \to +\infty$ as $u \to +\infty$. Hence, by theorem (3.3.2), the factor combination $\{\nu_1, \nu_2, \ldots, \nu_k\}$ is strong limitational.

QED.

From this theorem and theorem (3.2.16) one has the following corollary

(3.3.4) Corollary: Let the production structure be homothetic and satisfy $\phi.1$-$\phi.5$. If the production structure possesses the (*) property of theorem (3.2.16), a factor combination $\{\nu_1,\nu_2,\ldots,\nu_k\}$, $(1\leq k<n)$, is essential if and only if it is strong limitational.

A second condition, (beyond axioms $\phi.1$-$\phi.5$), sufficient to imply that a factor combination is strong limitational is stated next. But, first introduce:

(3.3.5) $$K(\bigcup_{u>0} E(u)) := \{x\varepsilon R^n_+ : y\varepsilon \bigcup_{u>0} E(u),\ x = \lambda\cdot y,\ \lambda > 0\},$$

the cone spanned by the union of efficient subsets for strictly positive output. Note that for a homothetic production structure, $K(\bigcup_{u>0} E(u)) = K(E(1))$. This is clear, since if $y\varepsilon \bigcup_{u>0} E(u)$, then by homotheticity, $y\varepsilon \bigcup_{u>0} F^{-1}(u)\cdot E(1)$, and for fixed u, $(y/F^{-1}(u))\ \varepsilon\ E(1)$.

(3.3.6) Theorem: (Färe, 1972) For a production structure satisfying axioms $\phi.1$-$\phi.5$, the existence of a closed cone $\overline{K(\bigcup_{u>0} E(u))}$ such that the intersection $(\overline{K(\bigcup_{u>0} E(u)} \cap D(\nu_1,\nu_2,\ldots,\nu_k))$ is empty is sufficient for a factor combination $\{\nu_1,\nu_2,\ldots,\nu_k\}$, $(1\leq k<n)$, to be strong limitational.

In proving theorem (3.3.6) the following lemma is useful.

(3.3.7) Lemma: Let $K\subset R^n_+$, $0\varepsilon K$ be a closed cone such that the intersection $K\cap D(\nu_1,\nu_2,\ldots,\nu_k)$, $(1\leq k<n)$, is empty. Then, for each positive bound B on the subvector $(x_{\nu_1},x_{\nu_2},\ldots,x_{\nu_k})$, the intersection $(K\cap\{x\varepsilon R^n_+ :\ ||\, x_{\nu_1},x_{\nu_2},\ldots,x_{\nu_k}\, || \leq B\})$ is

compact.

Proof: Let B be any positive bound on the subvector $(x_{\nu_1}, x_{\nu_2}, \ldots, x_{\nu_k})$ $(1 \leqq k < n)$, and define $S := (K \cap \{x \in R^n_+ : \| x_{\nu_1}, x_{\nu_2}, \ldots, x_{\nu_k} \| \leqq B\})$. The set S is closed as an intersection of two closed sets. Thus, it remains to be shown that S is bounded. Assume conversely that there is an infinite sequence $\{x^\ell\} \subset S$ such that $\| x^\ell \| \to +\infty$ as $\ell \to +\infty$. Since by assumption, the subvector $(x_{\nu_1}, x_{\nu_2}, \ldots, x_{\nu_k})$ is bounded, $\| x^\ell_{\nu_{k+1}}, x^\ell_{\nu_{k+2}}, \ldots, x^\ell_{\nu_n} \|$ must under these conditions tend to $+\infty$ as $\ell \to +\infty$. Now consider the sequence of rays $r^\ell := \{\lambda \cdot x^\ell : \lambda > 0\}$. $r^\ell \subset K$ for all ℓ and since K is closed $\lim_{\ell \to +\infty} r^\ell \in K$. It also follows from the boundedness of the subvector $(x_{\nu_1}, x_{\nu_2}, \ldots, x_{\nu_k})$ that $\lim_{\ell \to +\infty} r^\ell \in D(\nu_1, \nu_2, \ldots, \nu_k)$, contradicting the assumption that $K \cap D(\nu_1, \nu_2, \ldots, \nu_k)$ is empty. Hence S is a compact subset of R^n_+. Since the bound B was arbitrarily chosen, the lemma is proved.

QED.

Proof of theorem (3.3.6): By assumption, $(\overline{K(\bigcup_{u>0} E(u))} \cap D(\nu_1, \nu_2, \ldots, \nu_k))$ is empty. Therefore, for each positive bound, B, on the subvector $(x_{\nu_1}, x_{\nu_2}, \ldots, x_{\nu_k})$, the intersection $\overline{S} := (\overline{K(\bigcup_{u>0} E(u))} \cap \{x \in R^n_+ : \| x_{\nu_1}, x_{\nu_2}, \ldots, x_{\nu_k} \| \leqq B\})$ is compact. By axiom $\phi.5$ the production function is upper semi-continuous, therefore there is an x^o in this intersection such that $\phi(x^o) = \max\{\phi(x) : x \in \overline{S}\}$, see (6.B.5). Either $\phi(x^o) > 0$ or $\phi(x^o) = 0$. In the first case there is a $\lambda^o > 0$ such that $(L(\phi(\lambda^o \cdot x^o)) \cap \overline{S})$ is empty, see property L.2. Therefore, since $L(u) \subset (\overline{E(u)} + R^n_+)$ from theorem (2.4.4.), the intersection $L(\phi(\lambda^o \cdot x^o)) \cap \{x \in R^n_+ : \| x_{\nu_1}, x_{\nu_2}, \ldots, x_{\nu_k} \| \leqq B\}$ is empty and $\sup\{\phi(x) : x \in \{x \in R^n_+ : \| x_{\nu_1}, x_{\nu_2}, \ldots, x_{\nu_k} \| \leqq B\}\}$ is finite. In the case of $\phi(x^o) = 0$, choose another bound $\hat{B} > B$ such that $\phi(\overline{x}) = \max\{\phi(x) : x \in (\overline{K(\bigcup_{u>0} E(u))} \cap \{x \in R^n_+ : \| x_{\nu_1},$

$x_{\nu_2}, \ldots, x_{\nu_k} \| \leqq \hat{B}\})\}$ is positive and apply the argument for $\phi(x^o) > 0$. From property ϕ.4(a) it is clear that there is a required $\hat{B}$.

QED.

The sufficient condition in theorem (3.3.6) states that technically efficient factor substitution be uniformly, i.e., output independent, bounded away from $D(\nu_1, \nu_2, \ldots, \nu_k)$. To see that the condition in theorem (3.3.6) is not implied by strong limitationality, consider the following almost homogeneous Leontief production function.

(3.3.8) $\phi(x_1, x_2) := \min \{x_1, \sqrt{x_2}\}$.

The first factor is essential, and for each positive bound on that factor, output is bounded. Hence, x_1 is strong limitational. It can, however, easily be seen that $\lim_{u \to +\infty} r(u)$ belongs to $D(1)$, $r(u) := \{x \varepsilon R^2_+ : x = \lambda \cdot y, y \varepsilon \overline{E(u)}, \lambda > 0\}$. Thus, the sufficient condition stated in theorem (3.3.6) does not hold, yet still x_1 is strong limitational.

3.4 The Production Axioms and Bounded Output*

The next task is to establish minimal subsets of the production axioms under which theorems (3.2.9) and (3.3.6) still hold. This is accomplished by counterexamples.

Consider the second part of L.1. If this property does not hold, i.e., $\phi(0) > 0$, then no factor combination $\{\nu_1, \nu_2, \ldots, \nu_k\}$, $(1 \leq k < n)$, is essential, therefore weak limitationality does not imply essentiality.

Turning to property L.4(b), the following figure shows that theorem (3.2.9) cannot hold without this property.

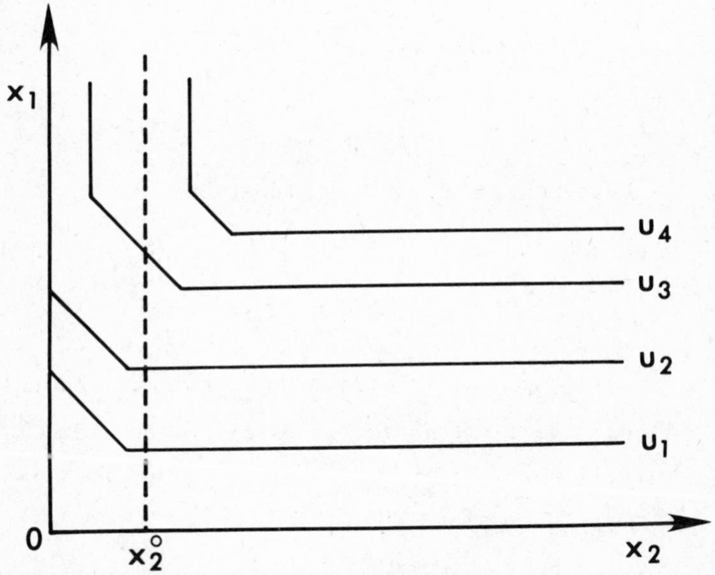

Figure 3.4.1

---

*This section is based on Shephard and Färe (1974).

For the input correspondence $u \to L(u)$ illustrated by figure 3.4.1, the second factor, x_2, is not essential. However, for the bound $x_2^0 > 0$, output is bounded by u_4. Hence, a nonessential factor combination is weak limitational, violating theorem (3.2.9).

Regarding property L.5, consider the input correspondence $u \to L(u)$ defined by:

$$(3.4.1) \qquad L(u) := \begin{cases} R_+^2 \text{ for } u = 0 \\ \{x \in R_+^2 : x_1 > 0,\ x_2 > 0,\ x_1 \cdot x_2 > u\} \\ \text{for } u > 0 \end{cases}$$

Clearly all properties L.1-L.7 but L.5 are satisfied for (3.4.1). Note that $E(u)$ is empty for $u > 0$ and therefore bounded. The first factor is essential since $L(u) \cap D(1)$ is empty for $u > 0$. However, if $x_1 > 0$, for each $u > 0$ there is some x_2 such that $x_1 \cdot x_2 > u$. Hence, x_1 is not weak limitational.

Next, consider a Cobb-Douglas production function:

$$(3.4.2) \qquad \phi(x_1, x_2) := A \cdot x_1^{\delta} \cdot x_2^{1-\delta}$$

where $A > 0$ and $0 < \delta < 1$. All axioms ϕ.1-ϕ.5 but ϕ.6, equivalent to L.7, are satisfied. The first factor is essential but not weak limitational, violating theorem (3.2.9).

Concerning property L.6, let the technology be as illustrated below.

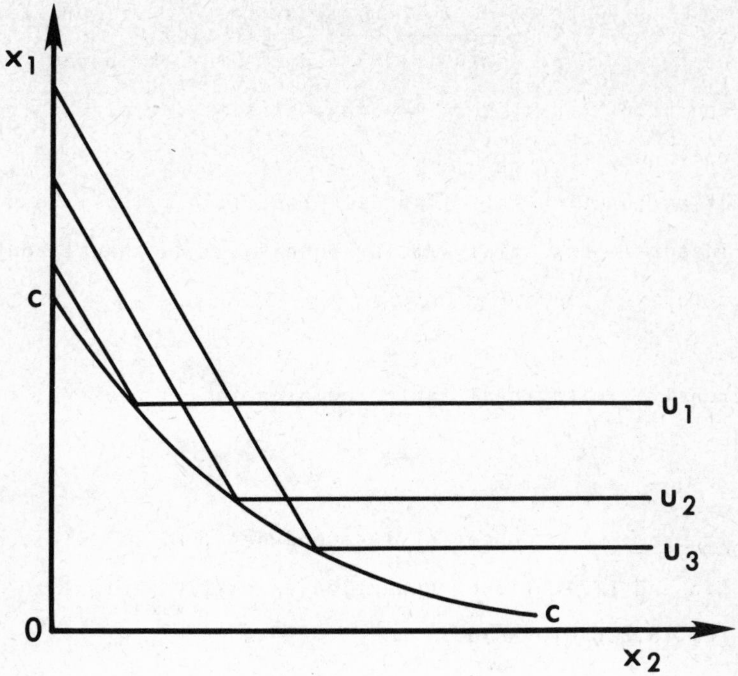

Figure 3.4.2

Here the efficient subsets are the straight line segments bounded by points on the x_1 axis and on the curve c - c asymptotic to the x_2 axis. The first factor is essential in this example, but there is no positive bound on it that in turn bounds output.

The above counterexamples prove:

(3.4.3) Theorem: The subset {L.1 second part, L.4(b), L.5, L.6 and L.7} of the production axioms, is minimal for theorem (3.2.9) to hold.

Finally, consider the production function

$$(3.4.4)\qquad \phi(x_1,x_2) := \begin{cases} \dfrac{1}{1-\min\{x_1,x_2\}} - 1 & \text{if } 0 \leqq \min\{x_1,x_2\} < 1, \\ +\infty & \text{if } \min\{x_1,x_2\} \geqq 1. \end{cases}$$

This production function satisfies all properties $\phi.1$-$\phi.6$ except $\phi.2$. The first factor is essential, yet for bounds greater than 1, output is not bounded for $x_2 \geqq 1$, violating theorem (3.3.6).

Since a strongly limitational factor combination is weakly limitational, one has:

(3.4.5) Theorem: The subset {L.1 second part, L.2, L.4(b), L.5, L.6 and L.7} of the production axioms, is minimal for theorem (3.3.6) to hold.

3.5 Law of Bounded Average Returns

Consider a two-input production function, ϕ, with $\phi(x_1,x_2) > 0$ and $x_2 > 0$, $x\varepsilon R^2_+$. If $x_2 \to \phi(x_1,x_2)/x_2$ is eventually decreasing, one refers to diminishing average returns to the second factor. For a comprehensive discussion of the law of diminishing average returns, see Eichhorn (1978). Here, a weaker law of average returns is analyzed, namely:

(3.5.1) Definition: There are Bounded Average Returns to the factor combination $\{\nu_{k+1},\nu_{k+2},\ldots,\nu_n\}$, $(1\leqq k<n)$, if for each fixed input vector $x^o\varepsilon R^n_+$ with $\phi(x^o) > 0$ and $(x^o_{\nu_{k+1}},x^o_{\nu_{k+2}},\ldots,x^o_{\nu_n}) > 0$, there is a scalar $\lambda^o \geqq 1$ such that $\phi(x^o_{\nu_1},x^o_{\nu_2},\ldots,x^o_{\nu_k}, \lambda\cdot x^o_{\nu_{k+1}},\ldots,\lambda\cdot x^o_{\nu_n}) \leqq \lambda\cdot\phi(x^o)$ for all $\lambda \geqq \lambda^o$.

If the factor combination $\{\nu_1,\nu_2,\ldots,\nu_k\}$ is strong limitational the following remark is valid.

(3.5.2) Remark: Let the production function satisfy $\phi.1$-$\phi.5$. If the factor combination $\{\nu_1,\nu_2,\ldots,\nu_k\}$, $(1\leqq k<n)$, is strong limitational, then there are bounded average returns to $\{\nu_{k+1},\nu_{k+2},\ldots,\nu_n\}$.

It is clear that requiring that $\{\nu_1,\nu_2,\ldots,\nu_k\}$ be strong limitational, is stronger than needed for bounded average returns to the factor combination $\{\nu_{k+1},\nu_{k+2},\ldots,\nu_n\}$. Actually, for this condition to apply, the factor combination $\{\nu_1,\nu_2,\ldots,\nu_k\}$ need not even be essential. This is illustrated by the production function:

(3.5.3) $\phi(x_1,x_2) = x_1 + x_2$.

Here the first factor is not essential, but there are bounded average returns to x_2. To elucidate this, let $x^o \varepsilon R^2_+$ with $x^o_2 > 0$. Take $\lambda \geqq 1$, then from (3.5.3),

(3.5.4) $\quad x^o_1 + \lambda \cdot x^o_2 \leqq \lambda \cdot x^o_1 + \lambda \cdot x^o_2 = \lambda \cdot (x^o_1 + x^o_2)$

showing that there are bounded average returns to x_2.

A second condition sufficient for bounded average returns to hold is next considered, namely:

(3.5.5) <u>Definition</u>: A factor combination $\{\nu_{k+1}, \nu_{k+2}, \ldots, \nu_n\}$, $(1 \leqq k < n)$, is Eventually Not Strong Disposable, if for some $x^o \varepsilon R^n_+$ with $(x^o_{\nu_{k+1}}, x^o_{\nu_{k+2}}, \ldots, x^o_{\nu_n}) > 0$ there is a $\lambda^o > 1$ such that $\phi(x^o_{\nu_1}, x^o_{\nu_2}, \ldots, x^o_{\nu_k}, \lambda^o \cdot x^o_{\nu_{k+1}}, \ldots, \lambda^o \cdot x^o_{\nu_n}) < \phi(x^o)$.

Definition (3.5.5) is illustrated by the production structure in figure 2.4.1.

(3.5.6) <u>Theorem</u>: Let the production structure satisfy $\phi.1$-$\phi.5$ and $\phi.8$. If the factor combination $\{\nu_{k+1}, \nu_{k+2}, \ldots, \nu_n\}$, $(1 \leqq k < n)$, is eventually not strong disposable, it has bounded average returns.

Proof: Since the factor combination $\{\nu_{k+1}, \nu_{k+2}, \ldots, \nu_n\}$ is eventually not strong disposable there is an $x^o \varepsilon R^n_+$ with $(x^o_{\nu_{k+1}}, x^o_{\nu_{k+2}}, \ldots, x^o_{\nu_n}) > 0$ and a $\lambda^o > 1$ such that $\phi(x^o_{\nu_1}, x^o_{\nu_2}, \ldots, x^o_{\nu_k}, \lambda^o \cdot x_{\nu_{k+1}} \ldots, \lambda^o \cdot x^o_{\nu_n}) < \phi(x^o)$. Since ϕ is quasi-concave and upper semi-continuous, there is a hyperplane (see (6.B.16)), strictly separating $L(\phi(x^o))$ and $(x^o_{\nu_1}, x^o_{\nu_2}, \ldots, x^o_{\nu_k}, \lambda^o \cdot x^o_{\nu_{k+1}}, \ldots, \lambda^o \cdot x^o_{\nu_n})$. Thus, since $L(u) \subset L(v)$ for all $u \geqq v$, it follows that $\phi(x^o_{\nu_1}, x^o_{\nu_2}, \ldots, x^o_{\nu_k}, \lambda \cdot x_{\nu_{k+1}}, \ldots, \lambda \cdot x^o_{\nu_n}) < \phi(x^o)$ for all

$\lambda \geqq \lambda^o$. Next, let $\hat{x}$ be any input vector with $(\hat{x}_{\nu_{k+1}}, \hat{x}_{\nu_{k+2}}, \ldots, \hat{x}_{\nu_n}) > 0$ yielding positive output $\phi(\hat{x})$. If $\phi(x^o) \geqq \phi(\hat{x})$ then $\phi(\hat{x}_{\nu_1}, \hat{x}_{\nu_2}, \ldots, \hat{x}_{\nu_k}, \lambda \cdot \hat{x}_{\nu_{k+1}}, \ldots, \lambda \cdot \hat{x}_{\nu_n})$ is bounded by $\phi(x^o)$. Thus, one need only consider $\phi(\hat{x}) > \phi(x^o)$. However, $(\hat{x}_{\nu_1}, \hat{x}_{\nu_2}, \ldots, \hat{x}_{\nu_k}, \lambda \cdot \hat{x}_{\nu_{k+1}}, \ldots, \lambda \cdot \hat{x}_{\nu_n})$ will intersect the above hyperplane for some $\lambda > 1$, and, therefore, there are bounded average returns to the factor combination $\{\nu_{k+1}, \nu_{k+2}, \ldots, \nu_n\}$.

QED.

Strong limitationality and eventually not strong disposability are properties on the production factors sufficient for bounded average returns to hold. Next, such conditions are derived for the case of a production function with two inputs. It is also assumed that the production function satisfies the following additional property.

(3.5.7) For $x \varepsilon R_+^2$ with $\phi(x) > 0$, $x_2 \to \phi(x_1, x_2)$ is continuous and strictly increasing.

The condition (3.5.7) is introduced as a mathematical condition to guarantee that ϕ has an inverse with respect to its second argument.

(3.5.8) Theorem: Let the production function $\phi: R_+^2 \to R_+$ satisfy ϕ.1-ϕ.5 and property (3.5.7). A necessary and sufficient condition for bounded average returns to the second factor ({2}), is that there exist a function $h: R_+^3 \to h(\lambda, x_1, x_2) \varepsilon R_+$, strictly increasing and continuous in λ, such that $h(\lambda, x_1, x_2) \geqq \lambda$ for all $\lambda \geqq 1$, and for each fixed $x^o \varepsilon R_+^2$ with $\phi(x^o) > 0$ and $x_2^o > 0$, $\phi(x_1^o, h(\lambda, x_1^o, x_2^o) \cdot x_2^o) = \lambda \cdot \phi(x^o)$, $\lambda \geqq \lambda^o$ for some $\lambda^o \geqq 1$.

Proof: Let $x^o \varepsilon R_+^2$ with $\phi(x^o) > 0$ and $x_2^o > 0$. Assume there is a function $h(\lambda, x_1^o, x_2^o)$ satisfying the conditions of the theorem. Then, since $h(\lambda, x_1^o, x_2^o) \geqq \lambda$ for $\lambda \geqq 1$, it follows from property (3.5.7) that $\lambda \cdot \phi(x_1^o, x_2^o) = \phi(x_1^o, h(\lambda, x_1^o, x_2^o) \cdot x_2^o) \geqq \phi(x_1^o, \lambda \cdot x_2^o)$ for $\lambda \geqq 1$. Hence, there are bounded average returns to the second factor.

To prove the converse, let $x^o \varepsilon R_+^2$ with $\phi(x^o) > 0$ and $x_2^o > 0$. Assume there are bounded average returns to the second factor, i.e., there is a $\lambda^o \geqq 1$ such that for all $\lambda \geqq \lambda^o$, $\phi(x_1^o, \lambda \cdot x_2^o) \leqq \lambda \cdot \phi(x_1^o, x_2^o)$. It now follows from (3.5.7) that

$$\lambda \leqq (x_2^o)^{-1} \cdot \phi^{-1}(x_1^o, \lambda \cdot \phi(x_1^o, x_2^o)).$$

Define $h(\lambda, x_1^o, x_2^o) := (x_2^o)^{-1} \cdot \phi^{-1}(x_1^o, \lambda \cdot \phi(x_1^o, x_2^o))$ and assume that $\phi(x_1^o, h(\lambda, x_1^o, x_2^o) \cdot x_2^o) > \lambda \cdot \phi(x_1^o, x_2^o)$ for some $\lambda > \lambda^o \geqq 1$.

Then, it follows from the definition of h that

$$\phi^{-1}(x_1^o, \lambda \cdot \phi(x_1^o, x_2^o)) > \phi^{-1}(x_1^o, \lambda \cdot \phi(x_1^o, x_2^o)),$$

a contradiction. Therefore, $\phi(x_1^o, h(\lambda, x_1^o, x_2^o) \cdot x_2^o) \leqq \lambda \cdot \phi(x_1^o, x_2^o)$. By reversing the inequality sign, one deduces that $\phi(x_1^o, h(\lambda, x_1^o, x_2^o) \cdot x_2^o) = \lambda \cdot \phi(x_1^o, x_2^o)$, $\lambda \geqq \lambda^o \geqq 1$. The required properties of h follow from those of ϕ.

QED.

In addition to the necessary and sufficient conditions for bounded average returns it is of interest to find the most general form of the function h satisfying the requirements of theorem (3.5.8). To pursue this issue, the following lemma is needed.

(3.5.9) Lemma: Let $f: A \to R_+$ where $A := \{(\lambda, x_1, x_2) \varepsilon R^3_+ : f(\lambda, x_1, x_2) > 0, \lambda > 0, x_i > 0, i = 1, 2\}$. The general solution to the functional equation

$$(3.5.10) \quad f(\lambda \cdot \mu, x_1, x_2) = f(\lambda, x_1, x_2) \cdot f(\mu, x_1, \lambda \cdot x_2) \text{ is}$$

$$f(\lambda, x_1, x_2) = \frac{g(x_1, \lambda \cdot x_2)}{g(x_1, x_2)}, \text{ where } g: A \to R_+ \text{ is an arbitrary}$$

function.

Proof:[1)] Substitute $\mu = 1/\lambda \cdot x_2$ into (3.5.10), then

$$(3.5.11) \quad f(\frac{1}{x_2}, x_1, x_2) = f(\lambda, x_1, x_2) \cdot f(\frac{1}{\lambda \cdot x_2}, x_1, \lambda \cdot x_2).$$

Define $g(x_1, x_2) := (f(\frac{1}{x_2}, x_1, x_2))^{-1}$ and $g(x_1, \lambda \cdot x_2) = (f(\frac{1}{\lambda \cdot x_2}, x_1, \lambda \cdot x_2))^{-1}$. It now follows from (3.5.11) that

$$(3.5.12) \quad f(\lambda, x_1, x_2) = \frac{g(x_1, \lambda \cdot x_2)}{g(x_1, x_2)}.$$

Let g be an arbitrary function $g: A \to R_+$ satisfying (3.5.12). The lemma now follows from substituting this into (3.5.10).

QED.

There is an interesting special case of (3.5.10), namely, $f(\mu, x_1, \lambda \cdot x_2) = f(\mu, x_1, x_2)$ for all $\lambda > 0$. If f is continuous in μ at a point, the general solution to

$$(3.5.13) \quad f(\lambda \cdot \mu, x_1, x_2) = f(\lambda, x_1, x_2) \cdot f(\mu, x_1, x_2)$$

is

[1)] This proof follows Eichhorn (1978), p. 211. Eichhorn gives additional references.

(3.5.14) $f(\lambda,x_1,x_2) = \lambda^{\alpha(x_1,x_2)}$, $\alpha(x_1,x_2) > 0$.

For proof see Eichhorn (1978) p. 23. However, since $f(\lambda,x_1,x_2) = f(\lambda,x_1,\mu\cdot x_2)$ for all $\mu > 0$, it follows that

(3.5.15) $f(\lambda,x_1,x_2) = \lambda^{\alpha(x_1)}$, $\alpha(x_1) > 0$.

With the above lemma, one can determine the most general form of h satisfying the conditions of theorem (3.5.8).

(3.5.16) Theorem: Let the production function $\phi: R_+^2 \to R_+$ satisfy $\phi.1$-$\phi.5$ and property (3.5.7). Let the function $h: R_+^3 \to R_+$ satisfy the conditions of theorem (3.5.8). The most general form of h is $h(\lambda,x_1,x_2) = g^{-1}(x_1,\lambda\cdot g(x_1,x_2))/x_2$, where g is an arbitrary function compatible with the assumptions on h.

Proof: Let $x^o \in R_+^2$ with $\phi(x^o) > 0$ and $x_2^o > 0$. Assume h satisfies the conditions of theorem (3.5.8). Then,

(3.5.17) $\phi(x_1^o,\ h(\lambda,x_1^o,x_2^o)\cdot x_2^o) = \lambda\cdot\phi(x_1^o,x_2^o)$

for $\lambda \geqq \lambda^o \geqq 1$. Note that without loss of generality, λ^o can be taken equal to one. Also, note that

(3.5.18) $h(1,x_1^o,x_2^o) = 1$.

Since h is strictly increasing and continuous in λ, define

(3.5.19) $\lambda := h^{-1}(\mu,x_1^o,x_2^o)$ for $\mu = h(\lambda,x_1^o,x_2^o) \geqq 1$.

Inserting (3.5.19) into (3.5.17) yields

$$(3.5.20) \qquad \phi(x_1^0,\mu\cdot x_2^0) = h^{-1}(\lambda,x_1^0,x_2^0) \cdot \phi(x_1^0,x_2^0).$$

Choose $\mu := \delta\cdot\rho$, $(\delta,\rho\geqq 1)$, then by (3.5.20),

$$(3.5.21) \qquad h^{-1}(\delta\cdot\rho,x_1^0,x_2^0) \cdot \phi(x_1^0,x_2^0) = h^{-1}(\delta,x_1^0,\rho\cdot x_2^0) \cdot \phi(x_1^0,\rho\cdot x_2^0).$$

Take $\delta = 1$ in (3.5.21) and use (3.5.18), then

$$(3.5.22) \qquad h^{-1}(\rho,x_1^0,x_2^0) \cdot \phi(x_1^0,x_2^0) = \phi(x_1^0,\rho\cdot x_2^0).$$

Insertion of (3.5.22) into (3.5.21) yields

$$(3.5.23) \qquad h^{-1}(\delta\cdot\rho,x_1^0,x_2^0) = h^{-1}(\rho,x_1^0,x_2^0) \cdot h^{-1}(\delta,x_1^0,\rho\cdot x_2^0).$$

The solution of the functional equation (3.5.23) is given by lemma (3.5.9) to be

$$(3.5.24) \qquad h^{-1}(\rho,x_1^0,x_2^0) = \frac{g(x_1^0,\rho\cdot x_2^0)}{g(x_1^0,x_2^0)}$$

where g is an arbitrary function. Here, strictly increasing and continuous in ρ since $h^{-1}(\rho,x_1^0,x_2^0)$ is strictly increasing and continuous in ρ. From (3.5.24) it follows that the most general form of h is

$$(3.5.25) \qquad h(\lambda,x_1,x_2) = g^{-1}(x_1,\lambda\cdot g(x_1,x_2))/x_2.$$

QED.

From theorems (3.5.8) and (3.5.16) it now follows that the most general production function for which there are bounded average returns to the second factor is

$$(3.5.26) \qquad \lambda \cdot \phi(x_1^0, x_2^0) = \phi(x_1^0, g^{-1}(x_1^0, \lambda \cdot g(x_1^0, x_2^0))),$$

where $(x_1^0, x_2^0) \varepsilon R_+^2$ and $g^{-1}(x_1^0, \lambda \cdot g(x_1^0, x_2^0))/x_2^0$ satisfy the conditions of theorems (3.5.8) and (3.5.16).

Finally, if the special form (3.5.15) applies, one has

$$(3.5.27) \qquad \lambda \cdot \phi(x_1^0, x_2^0) = \phi(x_1^0, \lambda^{\alpha(x_1^0)} \cdot x_2^0)$$

where $\alpha(x_1^0) > 0$.

4. CONGESTION, NULL JOINTNESS AND LAWS OF VARIABLE PROPORTIONS

4.1 Introduction*

The law of variable proportions, after Turgot (1767), is an intrinsic production property. In its simplest form, for a two-input technology, it states that as one factor is kept fixed, increases in the other factor first increase output, up to a maximum. Thereafter, output decreases. For sufficiently large amounts of the variable factor, output is zero.

In order to deduce this law from elementary properties on the factors of production, the notions of congestion among production factors and null jointness among inputs are introduced. Congestion is used here to mean that if some production factors are kept constant increases in the others may obstruct production. This concept is discussed in detail in sections 4.2 and 4.3. Technologies exhibiting congestion are frequently found in agriculture, engineering and transportation, therefore congestion is of importance in its own right. In addition, it is an important tool for deducing laws of variable proportions. Three form of congestion are defined in order to distinguish among different degrees of congestion. These forms are related to each other and to production theoretical concepts such as strong disposability of inputs and essentiality.

An important concept in the discussion of congestion and laws of variable proportions is null jointness among inputs. This notion expresses the idea that to achieve a positive output rate, certain requirements may have to be placed on the input mixes. In section 4.4,

---

*The contents of this chapter are modifications of (Färe and Jansson, 1976) and (Färe and Svensson, 1979).

jointness is defined and in section 4.5 it is related to the strongest form of congestion.

Two laws of variable proportions (after Turgot) are defined in section 4.6. Necessary and sufficient conditions on the production factors are stated for these laws to apply. The last section, 4.6, is devoted to an econometric example of an agricultural production process exhibiting a monotone law of variable proportions.

4.2 Congestion of Production Factors

Examples of production technologies exhibiting congestion in the sense that if a proper subset of factors of production is kept fixed, increases in the others may obstruct output, are frequently found in agriculture, transportation and engineering. To characterize such technologies, three forms of congestion among factors of production are defined.

(4.2.1) Definition: A factor combination $\{\nu_{k+1},\nu_{k+2},\ldots,\nu_n\}$, $(1 \leqq k<n)$, is Output-Limitational (OL- congested) at $x \varepsilon R^n_+$, if $\phi(x + y) \leqq \phi(x)$, for all $y \varepsilon D(\nu_1,\nu_2,\ldots,\nu_k)$. (See (3.2.1) for the definition of $D(\nu_1,\nu_2,\ldots,\nu_k)$).

If the factor combination $\{\nu_{k+1},\nu_{k+2},\ldots,\nu_n\}$ is OL- congested at $x \varepsilon R^n_+$, increases in those factors do not increase output. However, this does not say that output may decline due to such increases. Therefore, introduce:

(4.2.2) Definition: A factor combination $\{\nu_{k+1},\nu_{k+2},\ldots,\nu_n\}$, $(1 \leqq k<n)$, is Monotone Output-Limitational (MOL- congested) at $x \varepsilon R^n_+$, if $\phi(x + y'') \leqq \phi(x + y')$, for all $y' \varepsilon \overline{D}(\nu_1,\nu_2,\ldots,\nu_k)$ and $y'' \varepsilon D(\nu_1,\nu_2,\ldots,\nu_k)$ with $y' \leqq y''$.

This definition models the type of congestion that occurs when an increased application of the factor combination $\{\nu_{k+1},\nu_{k+2},\ldots,\nu_n\}$ not only bounds output, but also guarantees that output is nonincreasing under increased applications of $\{\nu_{k+1},\nu_{k+2},\ldots,\nu_n\}$.

Finally:

(4.2.3) <u>Definition</u>: A factor combination $\{\nu_{k+1},\nu_{k+2},\ldots,\nu_n\}$, $(1 \leqq k < n)$, is Output Prohibitive (OP- congested) at $x \varepsilon R_+^n$, if $\phi(x + y) = 0$, for all $y \varepsilon D(\nu_1,\nu_2,\ldots,\nu_k)$.

Here positive output is not possible when the factor combination $\{\nu_{k+1},\nu_{k+2},\ldots,\nu_n\}$ is increased. An empirical example of such a technology is discussed in section 4.7.

From the above three definitions it is clear that if a factor combination $\{\nu_{k+1},\nu_{k+2},\ldots,\nu_n\}$ is OP- congested at $x \varepsilon R_+^n$, it is MOL- congested there. Also, if $\{\nu_{k+1},\nu_{k+2},\ldots,\nu_n\}$ is MOL- congested at $x \varepsilon R_+^n$ it is OL- congested there. In general, however, the converse is not true. Hence the three definitions distinguish different degrees of congestion. Two examples of production functions clarify this.

(4.2.4) $\phi(x_1,x_2) := \min\{x_1,|2x_1 - x_2|\}$,

(4.2.5) $\phi(x_1,x_2) := \min\{x_1,x_2\}$.

In the first example, the production factor x_2 is OL- congested at $(x_1,x_2) = (1,0)$, but it is not MOL- congested at that point, since for $y'' = (0,2)$, $y' = (0,1)$, $\phi(x + y'') = 0 < \phi(x + y') = 1$.

For the production structure (4.2.5) with $x_1 = x_2 = 2$, it is clear that x_2 is MOL- congested at (2,2) but not OP- congested.

On the other hand, if the production technology exhibits strong disposability of inputs, i.e., if ϕ.3.S (equivalent to L.3.S) applies, then in definitions (4.2.1) and (4.2.2), the inequality sign may be replaced by equality and MOL- and OL- congestion coincide.

(4.2.6) Theorem: If a production function ϕ satisfies strong disposability of inputs (ϕ.3.S) in addition to ϕ.1-ϕ.5. Then a factor combination $\{\nu_{k+1}, \nu_{k+2}, \ldots, \nu_n\}$, $(1 \leqq k < n)$, is MOL-congested at $x \varepsilon R^n_+$ if and only if it is OL- congested at $x \varepsilon R^n_+$.

Proof: From the above discussion it is clearly sufficient to assume that the factor combination $\{\nu_{k+1}, \nu_{k+2}, \ldots, \nu_n\}$ is OL- congested at some $x \varepsilon R^n_+$ and to show that it is MOL- congested there. Under this assumption one has for $y' \varepsilon \bar{D}(\nu_1, \nu_2, \ldots, \nu_k)$ and $y'' \varepsilon D(\nu_1, \nu_2, \ldots, \nu_k)$ with $y'' \geqq y'$ that

$$\phi(x + y') \leqq \phi(x + y'') \leqq \phi(x + y')$$

proving the theorem.

QED.

To continue, consider the following subsets of factors of production:

(4.2.7) $OL(\nu_{k+1}, \nu_{k+2}, \ldots, \nu_n) := \{x \varepsilon R^n_+ : \{\nu_{k+1}, \nu_{k+2}, \ldots, \nu_n\}, (1 \leqq k < n),$ is OL- congested at $x\}$,

(4.2.8) $MOL(\nu_{k+1}, \nu_{k+2}, \ldots, \nu_n) := \{x \varepsilon R^n_+ : \{\nu_{k+1}, \nu_{k+2}, \ldots, \nu_n\}, (1 \leqq k < n),$ is MOL- congested at $x\}$,

(4.2.9) $OP(\nu_{k+1}, \nu_{k+2}, \ldots, \nu_n) := \{x \varepsilon R^n_+ : \{\nu_{k+1}, \nu_{k+2}, \ldots, \nu_n\}, (1 \leqq k < n),$ is OP- congested at $x\}$.

It is clear from the above discussion that $OP(\nu_{k+1}, \nu_{k+2}, \ldots, \nu_n) \subset MOL(\nu_{k+1}, \nu_{k+2}, \ldots, \nu_n) \subset OL(\nu_{k+1}, \nu_{k+2}, \ldots, \nu_n)$, and that $OL(\nu_{k+1}, \nu_{k+2}, \ldots, \nu_n) = MOL(\nu_{k+1}, \nu_{k+2}, \ldots, \nu_k) := \{x \varepsilon R^n_+ : \phi(x) = \phi(x + y)$ for all

$y \varepsilon D(v_1, v_2, \ldots, v_k)$, $(1 \leq k < n)\}$ whenever the production structure exhibits strong disposability of inputs.

It should also be noted, that under this disposability condition the set (4.2.9) may be nonempty with $OL(v_{k+1}, v_{k+2}, \ldots, v_n) \neq OP(v_{k+1}, v_{k+2}, \ldots, v_n)$. The following production function is an illustration of this case.

(4.2.10) $\phi(x_1, x_2) := \min \{\max \{0, x_1 - a\}, x_2\}$, $a > 0$.

Clearly this production function exhibits strong disposability of inputs, and, for $a = 1$, the input vector $(x_1, x_2) = (1,1)$ belongs to $OP(2)$. $(x_1, x_2) = (3,1)$ belongs to $OL(2)$ but $(3,1) \notin OP(2)$, i.e., $OP(2)$ is nonempty and $OP(2) \neq OL(2)$.

When only one factor is congested, i.e., $k=n-1$, it can be shown that if ϕ is a quasi-concave production function, then $OL(v_n) = MOL(v_n)$.

(4.2.11) <u>Theorem</u>: Let the production function be quasi-concave (i.e., $\phi.8$ applies) in addition to satisfy $\phi.1-\phi.5$. If $D(v_1, v_2, \ldots, v_k)$ is one-dimensional, i.e., $D(v_1, v_2, \ldots, v_k) = D(v_1, v_2, \ldots, v_{n-1})$, $OL(v_n) = MOL(v_n)$.

Proof: Since in general $MOL(v_n) \subset OL(v_n)$, it is sufficient to assume that $OL(v_n)$ is nonempty and to prove that $OL(v_n) \subset MOL(v_n)$. Hence, let $x \varepsilon OL(v_n)$ and let $y' \varepsilon \overline{D}(v_1, v_2, \ldots, v_{n-1})$ and $y'' \varepsilon D(v_1, v_2, \ldots, v_{n-1})$ with $y' \leq y''$. Since $D(v_1, v_2, \ldots, v_{n-1})$ has dimension one and $y' \leq y''$, $x + y'$ lies on the line segment between x and $x + y''$. By quasi-concavity, $\phi(x + y') \geq \min \{\phi(x), \phi(x + y'')\}$. Thus, since $\phi(x) \geq \phi(x + y')$, $(x \varepsilon OL(v_n))$, it follows that $\phi(x + y') \geq \phi(x + y'')$, i.e.,

$x \varepsilon MOL(\nu_n)$.

QED.

Unfortunately, as illustrated below, this theorem does not hold when there are more than one congested factor of production.

(4.2.12) $\phi(x_1,x_2,x_3) := \min\{x_1, \max\{0, x_2 - x_1 - x_3\}\}$.

The production function (4.2.12) is quasi-concave and it is next seen that the factor combination $\{x_2,x_3\}$ is OL- congested at $(x_1,x_2,x_3) = (1,3,1)$ but not MOL- congested there. From (4.2.12) it follows that

$$\phi(1, 3 + y_2, 1 + y_3) = \min\{1, \max\{0, 1 + y_2 - y_3\}\}$$
$$\leqq \phi(1,3,1) = 1$$

for all $y_i \geqq 0$, $i = 2,3$. Hence $\{x_2,x_3\}$ is OL- congested at the input vector (1,3,1). To see that $\{x_2,x_3\}$ is not MOL- congested there, choose (1,3,2) and (1,4,2). Then $\phi(1,3,2) = 0$ and $\phi(1,4,2) = 1$.

4.3 Properties of OL-, MOL- and OP- Congestion

In this section OL-, MOL- and OP- congestion are further investigated and these notions are related to other production theoretical concepts. First the relation between essentiality and OL- congestion is shown.

(4.3.1) Theorem: Let the production structure satisfy $\phi.1$-$\phi.5$. A factor combination $\{\nu_1,\nu_2,\ldots,\nu_k\}$, $(1 \leqq k<n)$, is essential if and only if $0 \varepsilon OL(\nu_{k+1},\nu_{k+2},\ldots,\nu_n)$.

Proof: Assume $0 \varepsilon OL(\nu_{k+1},\nu_{k+2},\ldots,\nu_n)$. Then $\phi(0 + y) \leqq \phi(0)$ for all $y \varepsilon D(\nu_1,\nu_2,\ldots,\nu_k)$ and by $\phi.1$ (i.e., $\phi(0) = 0$) the factor combination $\{\nu_1,\nu_2,\ldots,\nu_k\}$ is essential. Conversely, assume $\{\nu_1,\nu_2,\ldots,\nu_k\}$ essential. Then by $\phi.1$, $\phi(0 + y) = \phi(0) = 0$ for all $y \varepsilon D(\nu_1,\nu_2,\ldots,\nu_k)$ and hence $0 \varepsilon OL(\nu_{k+1},\nu_{k+2},\ldots,\nu_n)$.

QED.

Since by theorem (3.2.9) a factor combination is essential if and only if it is weak limitational, theorem (4.3.1) gives an alternative characterization of weak limitationality assuming that $\phi.6$ applies.

A further characterization of the condition $0 \varepsilon OL(\nu_{k+1},\nu_{k+2},\ldots,\nu_n)$ and hence of weak limitationality is next given for a quasi-concave production structure, namely:

(4.3.2) Theorem: Let the production structure satisfy $\phi.1$-$\phi.5$ in addition to be quasi-concave, i.e., $\phi.8$ applies. If $\phi(x) > 0$ for some $x \varepsilon OL(\nu_{k+1},\nu_{k+2},\ldots,\nu_n)$ then $0 \varepsilon OL(\nu_{k+1},\nu_{k+2},\ldots,\nu_n)$, $(1 \leqq k<n)$.

Proof: Let $x^0 \varepsilon OL(\nu_{k+1},\nu_{k+2},\ldots,\nu_n)$ with $\phi(x^0) > 0$, and consider the set $(\{x\varepsilon R^n_+ : \phi(x) \geqq \phi(x^0)\} \cap D(\nu_1,\nu_2,\ldots,\nu_k))$, $(1 \leqq k<n)$. If this intersection is empty, then by property $\phi.4(b)$, $\phi(y) = 0$ for all $y\varepsilon D(\nu_1,\nu_2,\ldots,\nu_k)$ and hence the factor combination $\{\nu_1,\nu_2,\ldots,\nu_k\}$ is essential. Thus by theorem (4.3.1), $0\varepsilon OL(\nu_{k+1},\nu_{k+2},\ldots,\nu_n)$. If on the other hand the intersection is not empty, it contains a z^0 with $\phi(z^0) > 0$. From the condition $x^0 \varepsilon OL(\nu_{k+1},\nu_{k+2},\ldots,\nu_n)$, it follows that $\phi(x^0) \geqq \phi(x^0 + z^0)$ and since $z^0\varepsilon D(\nu_1,\nu_2,\ldots,\nu_k)$, $\phi(x^0 + z^0) \geqq \phi(x^0 + \lambda\cdot z^0)$ for $\lambda \geqq 1$. From quasi-concavity of ϕ one has

$$\phi(x^0 + \lambda\cdot z^0) = \phi\left(\frac{1}{2^\ell}\cdot(2^\ell\cdot x^0) + \frac{2^\ell-1}{2^\ell}\cdot\frac{2^\ell\cdot\lambda\cdot z^0}{2^\ell-1}\right)$$

$$\geqq \min\left\{\phi(2^\ell\cdot x^0),\ \phi\left(\frac{2^\ell\cdot\lambda\cdot z^0}{2^\ell-1}\right)\right\}$$

for each $\ell = 1,2,\ldots,$. Since $\phi(z^0) > 0$, $\phi(\frac{2^\ell\cdot\lambda\cdot z^0}{2^\ell-1}) > 0$ for each $\lambda \geqq \frac{2^\ell-1}{2^\ell}$. Hence by property $\phi.4(b)$ of the production structure, for each ℓ there is a scalar $\bar{\lambda}(\ell)$ such that

$$\min\ \{\phi(2^\ell\cdot x^0),\ \phi(\frac{2^\ell\cdot\bar{\lambda}(\ell)\cdot z^0}{2^\ell-1})\} = \phi(2^\ell\cdot x^0).$$

Consequently, $\phi(x^0) \geqq \phi(2^\ell\cdot x^0)$ for all $\ell = 1,2\ldots,$. However, $\phi(x^0)$ is positive and bounded (see $\phi.2$) and therefore property $\phi.4(b)$ implies that $\phi(2^\ell\cdot x^0)\to+\infty$ as $\ell\to+\infty$, contradicting the condition $\phi(x^0) \geqq \phi(2^\ell\cdot x^0)$ for all $\ell = 1,2,\ldots$. Consequently the intersection $(\{x\varepsilon R^n_+ : \phi(x) \geqq \phi(x^0)\} \cap D(\nu_1,\nu_2,\ldots,\nu_k))$ is empty and by the above arguments, $0\varepsilon OL(\nu_{k+1},\nu_{k+2},\ldots,\nu_n)$.

QED.

Theorem (4.3.2) is essential in the discussion of OP- congestion and null jointness of inputs. It is therefore of importance to show the necessity of quasi-concavity and the condition $\phi(x) > 0$ for some

$x \varepsilon OL(\nu_{k+1}, \nu_{k+2}, \ldots, \nu_n)$ for the theorem to hold. Let

$$(4.3.3) \quad \phi(x_1,x_2) := \begin{cases} x_1 \text{ for } x_1 \geqq 0,\ x_2 = 0 \\ x_2 \text{ for } x_1 = 0,\ x_2 \geqq 0 \\ 0 \text{ otherwise} \end{cases}$$

$\phi(x_1,x_2)$ is a production function, it satisfies $\phi.1$-$\phi.5$, but it is not quasi-concave. However, $(x_1,x_2) = (1,0) \varepsilon OL(2)$ and $\phi(1,0) = 1$ so the condition $\phi(x) > 0$ for some $x \varepsilon OL(2)$ is fulfilled. The second factor is clearly OL- congested at $(x_1,x_2) = (1,1)$ but not at $(0,0)$, showing that theorem (4.3.2) does not hold in general without the assumption of quasi-concavity of ϕ.

Modify example (4.3.3) to read:

$$(4.3.4) \quad \phi(x_1,x_2) := \begin{cases} x_2 \text{ for } x_1 = 0,\ x_2 \geqq 0 \\ \text{and} \\ 0 \text{ otherwise.} \end{cases}$$

This production function is quasi-concave in addition to satisfy $\phi.1$-$\phi.5$. However, for all $(x_1,x_2) \varepsilon OL(1) = \{x \varepsilon R^2_+ : x_1 > 0,\ x_2 \geqq 0\}$, $\phi(x_1,x_2) = 0$, showing that the second requirement of theorem (4.3.2) is not fulfilled, and $(0,0) \notin OL(1)$.

The production structure (4.3.4) exemplifies the case when one input, here x_1, "poisons" output. Such models are important in discussions of external diseconomies.

As for MOL- and OP- congestion, note that

(4.3.5) $OP(\nu_{k+1},\nu_{k+2},\ldots,\nu_n) \cap \phi^{-1}(0) = MOL(\nu_{k+1},\nu_{k+2},\ldots,\nu_n) \cap \phi^{-1}(0)$
$= OL(\nu_{k+1},\nu_{k+2},\ldots,\nu_n) \cap \phi^{-1}(0)$,

where $\phi^{-1}(0) := \{x \varepsilon R^n_+ : \phi(x) = 0\}$, proving:

(4.3.6) <u>Theorem</u>: $0 \varepsilon OP(\nu_{k+1},\nu_{k+2},\ldots,\nu_n)$ if and only if $0 \varepsilon MOL(\nu_{k+1},\nu_{k+2},\ldots,\nu_n)$ if and only if $0 \varepsilon OL(\nu_{k+1},\nu_{k+2},\ldots,\nu_n)$.

From this theorem, it is evident that in theorems (4.3.1) and (4.3.2) the set $OL(\nu_{k+1},\nu_{k+2},\ldots,\nu_n)$ can be replaced by $MOL(\nu_{k+1},\nu_{k+2},\ldots,\nu_n)$ or $OP(\nu_{k+1},\nu_{k+2},\ldots,\nu_n)$.

For the special case of a homothetic production structure it is now shown that if there are OL- congested input vectors, these form a cone. This theorem is used in the discussion of laws of variable proportions.

Assume $x^o \varepsilon OL(\nu_{k+1},\nu_{k+2},\ldots,\nu_n)$, $(1 \leqq k < n)$. Then for all $y \varepsilon D(\nu_1,\nu_2,\ldots,\nu_k)$, $F(\psi(1, x^o + y)) \leqq F(\psi(1,x^o))$, where $\phi(x) := F(\psi(1,x))$ is a homothetic production function, (see (2.5.2)). From homogeneity of ψ it is clear that $\psi(1, \lambda \cdot x^o + \lambda \cdot y) \leqq \psi(1, \lambda \cdot x^o)$ and since $D(\nu_1,\nu_2,\ldots,\nu_k)$ is a cone, $F(\psi(\lambda \cdot x^o + \tilde{y})) \leqq F(\psi(1, \lambda \cdot x^o))$, $\lambda > 0$ and $\tilde{y} \varepsilon D(\nu_1,\nu_2,\ldots,\nu_k)$, implying that $\lambda \cdot x^o \varepsilon OL(\nu_{k+1},\nu_{k+2},\ldots,\nu_n)$ or that the OL- congested input vectors form a cone. Similar proofs apply for the sets $MOL(\nu_{k+1},\nu_{k+2},\ldots,\nu_n)$ and $OP(\nu_{k+1},\nu_{k+2},\ldots,\nu_n)$. Thus, one has:

(4.3.7) <u>Theorem</u>: Let the production structure be homothetic and $OL(\nu_{k+1},\nu_{k+2},\ldots,\nu_n)$, $(1 \leqq k < n)$, $(MOL(\nu_{k+1},\nu_{k+2},\ldots,\nu_n)$, $OP(\nu_{k+1},\nu_{k+2},\ldots,\nu_n))$ be nonempty, then $OL(\nu_{k+1},\nu_{k+2},\ldots,\nu_n)$ $(MOL(\nu_{k+1},\nu_{k+2},\ldots,\nu_n)$, $OP(\nu_{k+1},\nu_{k+2},\ldots,\nu_n))$ is a cone.

4.4 Null Joint Factors of Production

To express the idea that for positive output certain requirements may have to be placed on input mixes, the notion of null jointness among production factors is introduced. This notion plays an important role for the laws of variable proportions discussed in section 4.6. Formally:

(4.4.1) Definition: A factor combination $\{\nu_{k+1},\nu_{k+2},\dots,\nu_\ell\}$, $(1 \leqq k<\ell \leqq n)$, is Null Joint with $\{\nu_1,\nu_2,\dots,\nu_k\}$ if $(x_{\nu_1},x_{\nu_2},\dots,x_{\nu_k}) = 0$ implies $(x_{\nu_{k+1}},x_{\nu_{k+2}},\dots,x_{\nu_\ell}) = 0$ for $x \varepsilon \overline{C(1)}$ (see (2.4.7) for the definition of C(1)).

This definition states that if x belongs to the closed cone spanned by L(1), i.e., the cone containing those input vectors yielding positive output, with the subvector $(x_{\nu_1},x_{\nu_2},\dots,x_{\nu_k}) = 0$, then $(x_{\nu_{k+1}},x_{\nu_{k+2}},\dots,x_{\nu_\ell})$ is also zero. Hence, for positive production, $(x_{\nu_1},x_{\nu_2},\dots,x_{\nu_k})$ must be semi-positive.

A useful characterization of null jointness between a proper subset of factors and its complement is:

(4.4.2) Theorem: The factor combination $\{\nu_{k+1},\nu_{k+2},\dots,\nu_n\}$, $(1 \leqq k<n)$, is null joint with $\{\nu_1,\nu_2,\dots,\nu_k\}$ if and only if $\overline{C(1)} \cap D(\nu_1,\nu_2,\dots,\nu_k)$ is empty.

Proof: Assume $x \varepsilon \overline{C(1)} \cap D(\nu_1,\nu_2,\dots,\nu_k)$, then the subvector $(x_{\nu_1},x_{\nu_2},\dots,x_{\nu_k}) = 0$ and $(x_{\nu_{k+1}},x_{\nu_{k+2}},\dots,x_{\nu_n}) \geq 0$. Thus $\{\nu_{k+1},\nu_{k+2},\dots,\nu_n\}$ is not null joint with the factor combination $\{\nu_1,\nu_2,\dots,\nu_k\}$. Conversely, assume that $\{\nu_{k+1},\nu_{k+2},\dots,\nu_n\}$ is not null joint with $\{\nu_1,\nu_2,\dots,\nu_k\}$, then there is an $x \varepsilon \overline{C(1)}$ with the subvector $(x_{\nu_1},x_{\nu_2},\dots,$

$x_{\nu_k}) = 0$ and $(x_{\nu_{k+1}}, x_{\nu_{k+2}}, \ldots, x_{\nu_n}) \geq 0$. Thus, $x \varepsilon D(\nu_1, \nu_2, \ldots, \nu_k)$ and the intersection $(\overline{C(1)} \cap D(\nu_1, \nu_2, \ldots, \nu_k))$ is not empty.

QED.

Null jointness between factor combinations is not necessarily symmetric, thus introduce:

(4.4.3) Definition: The factor combinations $\{\nu_1, \nu_2, \ldots, \nu_k\}$, $(1 \leqq k < \ell \leqq n)$, and $\{\nu_{k+1}, \nu_{k+2}, \ldots, \nu_\ell\}$ are Symmetric Null Joint if and if $(x_{\nu_1}, x_{\nu_2}, \ldots, x_{\nu_k}) = 0$ if and only if $(x_{\nu_{k+1}}, x_{\nu_{k+2}}, \ldots, x_{\nu_\ell}) = 0$ for $x \varepsilon \overline{C(1)}$.

The following corollary to theorem (4.4.2) elucidates symmetric null jointness.

(4.4.4) Corollary: The factor combinations $\{\nu_1, \nu_2, \ldots, \nu_k\}$, $(1 \leqq k < \ell \leqq n)$, and $\{\nu_{k+1}, \nu_{k+2}, \ldots, \nu_\ell\}$ are symmetric null joint if and only if $D(\nu_1, \nu_2, \ldots, \nu_k) \cap \overline{C(1)} = D(\nu_{k+1}, \nu_{k+2}, \ldots, \nu_\ell) \cap \overline{C(1)}$ empty.

Consider the WDI production function (2.5.9) with β_1 and $\beta_2 > 0$, $\rho \varepsilon (-1, 0)$ (in addition to the other restrictions on its parameters):

$$(4.4.5) \quad \phi(x_1, x_2) := \begin{cases} A \cdot [\delta \cdot (x_1 - \beta_2 \cdot x_2)^{-\rho} + (1-\delta) \cdot (x_2 - \beta_1 \cdot x_1)^{-\rho}]^{-1/\rho} \\ \text{if } (x_i - \beta_j \cdot x_j) \geqq 0, \ i \neq j, \ i,j = 1,2 \\ 0 \text{ otherwise.} \end{cases}$$

In this case, clearly $\overline{C(1)} \cap D(1) = \overline{C(1)} \cap D(2)$, hence the two factors are symmetric null joint. In the case $\beta_1 > 0$ and $\beta_2 = 0$, x_1 is null joint with x_2 and for $\beta_1 = 0$, $\beta_2 > 0$ the converse holds.

It was shown in section 2.4 that if a production structure exhibits strong disposability of inputs, then $\overline{C(1)} = R^n_+$, (see theorem (2.4.8)). Thus, from the definition of null jointness the following is true.

(4.4.6) Corollary: If the production structure satisfies ϕ.1-ϕ.5 and ϕ.3.S, then no factor combination $\{\nu_1,\nu_2,\ldots,\nu_k\}$ is null joint with any other combination $\{\nu_{k+1},\nu_{k+2},\ldots,\nu_\ell\}$, $(1 \leqq k < \ell \leqq n)$.

It was shown in section 2.4 that if ϕ satisfies ϕ.1-ϕ.5 and is quasi-concave, then $\overline{C(1)} = R^n_+$ implies that inputs are strongly disposable, see theorem (2.4.9). Therefore, one has:

(4.4.7) Corollary: Let the production structure satisfy ϕ.1-ϕ.5, ϕ.8 and let no factor combination be null joint with any other, then inputs are strongly disposable.

The following simple corollaries, stated without proofs, show two relationships between null jointness and essentiality.

(4.4.8) Corollary: If a factor combination $\{\nu_{k+1},\nu_{k+2},\ldots,\nu_n\}$, $(1 \leqq k < n)$, is null joint with $\{\nu_1,\nu_2,\ldots,\nu_k\}$, then $\{\nu_1,\nu_2,\ldots,\nu_k\}$ is essential.

(4.4.9) Corollary: If a factor combination $\{\nu_{k+1},\nu_{k+2},\ldots,\nu_\ell\}$, $(1 \leqq k < \ell \leqq n)$, is essential and null joint with $\{\nu_1,\nu_2,\ldots,\nu_k\}$, then $\{\nu_1,\nu_2,\ldots,\nu_k\}$ is essential.

The cone $K(\bigcup_{u>0} E(u))$ defined in (3.3.5) was used in section 3.3 to show when a factor combination is strong limitational. Clearly, from definitions (2.4.7) and (3.3.5), $\overline{K(\bigcup_{u>0} E(u))}$ is contained in $\overline{C(1)}$.

It therefore follows from theorem (3.3.6):

(4.4.10) Corollary: Let the production structure satisfy ϕ.1-ϕ.5. If the factor combination $\{\nu_{k+1},\nu_{k+2},\ldots,\nu_n\}$, $(1 \leqq k<n)$, is null joint with $\{\nu_1,\nu_2,\ldots,\nu_k\}$, then $\{\nu_1,\nu_2,\ldots,\nu_k\}$ is strong limitational.

Finally, as a consequence of lemma (3.3.7) and property ϕ.5 on the production structure, corollary (4.4.10) can be strengthened to read:

(4.4.11) Theorem: Let the production structure satisfy ϕ.1-ϕ.5. If the factor combination $\{\nu_{k+1},\nu_{k+2},\ldots,\nu_n\}$, $(1 \leqq k<n)$, is null joint with $\{\nu_1,\nu_2,\ldots,\nu_k\}$, then for each positive bound B on the subvector $(x_{\nu_1},x_{\nu_2},\ldots,x_{\nu_k})$, ϕ achieves a maximum on the set $\{x\varepsilon R^n_+ : \| x_{\nu_1},x_{\nu_2},\ldots,x_{\nu_k} \| \leqq B\}$.

Proof: It follows from lemma (3.3.7) that the intersection $(\overline{C(1)} \cap \{x\varepsilon R^n_+ : \| x_{\nu_1},x_{\nu_2},\ldots,x_{\nu_k} \| \leqq B\})$ is compact and hence ϕ achieves a maximum, on this set (see (6.B.4)). Since $\phi(x) = 0$ on the complement of this set, the theorem is proved.

QED.

If the production function, in addition to satisfy properties ϕ.1-ϕ.5 is concave, it is next shown that $R^n_+ = \overline{C(1)}$. Hence, under these conditions no factor combination is null joint with any other.

(4.4.12) Theorem: Let the production function satisfy ϕ.1-ϕ.5 and let it be concave on R^n_+. Then, $\overline{C(1)} = R^n_+$.

Proof: Assume that $\overline{C(1)} \neq R^n_+$, then $(R^n_+ \setminus \overline{C(1)})$ is an open set. Thus, there exists an $x^0 \varepsilon (R^n_+ \setminus \overline{C(1)})$ and an $\varepsilon > 0$ such that the open sphere $S_\varepsilon(x^0) = \{x\varepsilon R^n_+ : \| x - x^0 \| < \varepsilon\}$ belongs to $(R^n_+ \setminus \overline{C(1)})$. Note that since $S_\varepsilon(x^o) \subset (R^n_+ \setminus \overline{C(1)})$, $\phi(x) = 0$ for all $x \varepsilon S_\varepsilon(x^o)$. Let $y \varepsilon L(1)$ and consider $\phi((1-\delta)x^o + \delta \cdot y)$, $0 \leqq \delta \leqq 1$. For $\delta = 0$ this expression is zero and for $\delta = 1$ it is strictly positive. Since $\varepsilon > 0$, there is a $\hat{\delta} > 0$ such that $\phi((1-\hat{\delta}) \cdot x^o + \hat{\delta} \cdot y) = 0$. Hence, $\phi((1-\hat{\delta}) \cdot x^o + \hat{\delta} \cdot y) = 0 < (1-\hat{\delta})\phi(x^o) + \hat{\delta} \cdot \phi(y)$, contradicting concavity of ϕ. (For the definition of concavity see (6.B.17)).

QED.

4.5 OP- Congested and Null Joint Factors of Production

In this section relationships between OP- congested and null joint factor combinations are proved. These theorems are important for the laws of variable proportions discussed in the following section. First one has:

(4.5.1) Theorem: Let the production structure satisfy $\phi.1$-$\phi.5$ and $\phi.8$. A factor combination $\{\nu_{k+1},\nu_{k+2},\ldots,\nu_n\}$, $(1\leqq k<n)$, is null joint with $\{\nu_1,\nu_2,\ldots,\nu_k\}$ if and only if there is an input vector $x^o\varepsilon\ OP(\nu_{k+1},\nu_{k+2},\ldots,\nu_n)$ such that $\phi(z^o) > 0$ for some $z^0 := x^0 - y^0$, where $y^0\varepsilon D(\nu_1,\nu_2,\ldots,\nu_k)$ and $(\{x\varepsilon R^n_+: \|x\| > \|x^0\|\}\cap\{x\varepsilon R^n_+: (x_{\nu_1},x_{\nu_2},\ldots,x_{\nu_k}) = (x^o_{\nu_1},x^o_{\nu_2},\ldots,x^o_{\nu_k})\})\subset OP(\nu_{k+1},\nu_{k+2},\ldots,\nu_n)$.

Proof: Assume first that the factor combination $\{\nu_{k+1},\nu_{k+2},\ldots,\nu_n\}$, $(1\leqq k<n)$, is null joint with $\{\nu_1,\nu_2,\ldots,\nu_k\}$. By theorem (4.4.2) the intersection $(\overline{C(1)}\cap D(\nu_1,\nu_2,\ldots,\nu_k))$ is empty (see (2.4.7) and (3.2.1) for definitions of $\overline{C(1)}$ and $D(\nu_1,\nu_2,\ldots,\nu_k)$ respectively). By property $\phi.4$(a), there is an input vector $z^0\varepsilon\overline{C(1)}$ such that $\phi(z^0) > 0$. It now follows from lemma (3.3.7) that there is an input vector $x^0\varepsilon$ $OP(\nu_{k+1},\nu_{k+2},\ldots,\nu_n)$ given by $x^0 := z^0 + y^0$, for some $y^0\varepsilon D(\nu_1,\nu_2,\ldots,\nu_k)$ and that $(\{x\varepsilon R^n_+: \|x\| > \|x^0\|\}\cap\{x\varepsilon R^n_+: (x_{\nu_1},x_{\nu_2},\ldots,x_{\nu_k}) = (x^o_{\nu_1},x^o_{\nu_2},\ldots,x^o_{\nu_k})\})\subset OP(\nu_{k+1},\nu_{k+2},\ldots,\nu_n)$ proving the first part.

To prove the converse, assume there is an input vector $x^0\varepsilon OP(\nu_{k+1},\nu_{k+2},\ldots,\nu_n)$ such that $\phi(z^o) > 0$ for some $z^0 := x^0 - y^0$, where $y^0\varepsilon D(\nu_1,\nu_2,\ldots,\nu_k)$ and that $(\{x\varepsilon R^n_+: \|x\| > \|x^0\|\}\cap\{x\varepsilon R^n_+: (x_{\nu_1},x_{\nu_2},\ldots,x_{\nu_k}) = (x^o_{\nu_1},x^o_{\nu_2},\ldots,x^o_{\nu_k})\})\subset OP(\nu_{k+1},\nu_{k+2},\ldots,\nu_n)$. The intersection $F := (\{x\varepsilon R^n_+: \|x\| \leqq \|x^0\|\}\cap\{x\varepsilon R^n_+: (x_{\nu_1},x_{\nu_2},\ldots,x_{\nu_k}) = (x^o_{\nu_1},x^o_{\nu_2},\ldots,x_{\nu_k})\})$ is compact and since ϕ is upper semi-continuous, (see $\phi.5$), there is an input vector $x^* \varepsilon F$ such that $\phi(x^*) = \max\{\phi(x): x \varepsilon F\}$, (see (6.B.4)). Thus $x^* \varepsilon OL(\nu_{k+1}, \nu_{k+2}, \ldots, \nu_n)$. Therefore, by theorems (4.3.2) and (4.3.6), $0 \varepsilon OP(\nu_{k+1}, \nu_{k+2}, \ldots, \nu_n)$. Moreover, $D(\nu_1, \nu_2, \ldots, \nu_k) \subset OP(\nu_{k+1}, \nu_{k+2}, \ldots, \nu_n)$ and hence by ϕ.3, the intersection $(\{x \varepsilon R^n_+: \| x \| > \| x^0 \|\} \cap \{x \varepsilon R^n_+: (x_{\nu_1}, x_{\nu_2}, \ldots, x_{\nu_k}) \leqq (x^o_{\nu_1}, x^o_{\nu_2}, \ldots, x^o_{\nu_k})\})$ belongs to $OP(\nu_{k+1}, \nu_{k+2}, \ldots, \nu_n)$. From this and the fact that $\overline{C(1)} = \overline{C(u)}$, for $u > 0$, it follows that $(\overline{C(1)} \cap D(\nu_1, \nu_2, \ldots, \nu_k))$ is empty. Hence, by theorem (4.4.2) the factor combination $\{\nu_{k+1}, \nu_{k+2}, \ldots, \nu_n\}$ is null joint with $\{\nu_1, \nu_2, \ldots, \nu_k\}$.

QED.

In theorem (4.5.1) the convexity assumption, ϕ.8, is used to guarantee that $0 \varepsilon OP(\nu_{k+1}, \nu_{k+2}, \ldots, \nu_n)$ when there is an input vector $x^0 \varepsilon OP(\nu_{k+1}, \nu_{k+2}, \ldots, \nu_n)$ such that $\phi(z^0) > 0$ for some $z^0 := x^0 - y^0$, where $y^0 \varepsilon D(\nu_1, \nu_2, \ldots, \nu_k)$, suggesting a second relationship between null jointness and OP- congestion.

(4.5.2) Theorem: Let the production structure satisfy ϕ.1-ϕ.5 in addition to be homothetic. A factor combination $\{\nu_{k+1}, \nu_{k+2}, \ldots, \nu_n\}$, $(1 \leqq k < n)$, is null joint with $\{\nu_1, \nu_2, \ldots, \nu_k\}$ if and only if $0 \varepsilon OP(\nu_{k+1}, \nu_{k+2}, \ldots, \nu_n)$ and there is an input vector $x^0 \varepsilon OP(\nu_{k+1}, \nu_{k+2}, \ldots, \nu_n)$ such that $\phi(z^0) > 0$ for some $z^0 := x^0 - y^0$, where $y^0 \varepsilon D(\nu_1, \nu_2, \ldots, \nu_k)$ and $(\{x \varepsilon R^n_+: \| x \| > \| x^0 \|\} \cap \{x \varepsilon R^n_+: (x_{\nu_1}, x_{\nu_2}, \ldots, x_{\nu_k}) = (x^o_{\nu_1}, x^o_{\nu_2}, \ldots, x_{\nu_k})\}) \subset OP(\nu_{k+1}, \nu_{k+2}, \ldots, \nu_n)$.

Proof: Assume the factor combination $\{\nu_{k+1}, \nu_{k+2}, \ldots, \nu_n\}$, $(1 \leqq k < n)$, is null joint with $\{\nu_1, \nu_2, \ldots, \nu_k\}$. By corollary (4.4.8) it is essential and by theorems (4.3.1) and (4.3.6), $0 \varepsilon OP(\nu_{k+1}, \nu_{k+2}, \ldots, \nu_n)$. The rest of this part of the proof follows like the proof of theorem

(4.5.1), and is deleted.

To prove the converse, note that, like in the proof of theorem (4.5.1) the intersection $(\{x \varepsilon R_+^n : \| x \| > \| x^o \|\} \cap \{x \varepsilon R_+^n : (x_{\nu_1}, x_{\nu_2}, \ldots, x_{\nu_k}) \leqq (x^o_{\nu_1}, x^o_{\nu_2}, \ldots, x^o_{\nu_k})\})$ belongs to $OP(\nu_{k+1}, \nu_{k+2}, \ldots, \nu_n)$. Therefore, by theorem (4.3.7), $(\overline{C(1)} \cap D(\nu_1, \nu_2, \ldots, \nu_k))$ is empty and hence by theorem (4.4.2), this theorem is true.

QED.

4.6 Laws of Variable Proportions

Consider the following illustration of a two-factor production technology $\phi(x_1, x_2)$, where the first factor is kept constant while the second may vary.

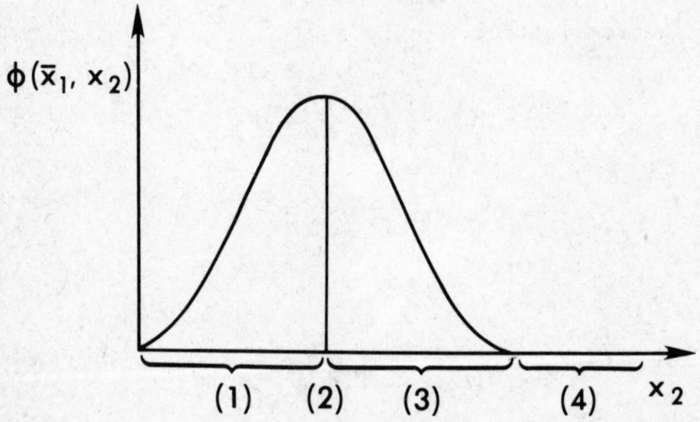

Figure 4.6.1

Four phases are distinguished. The first (1) when output is increasing, the second (2) where it reaches its maximum and the third (3) when output decreases with increases of x_2, and the fourth (4) where output is zero.

Over the four regions the factor proportion (x_1/x_2) is changing and production variation like this has become known as a law of variable proportions after Turgot, (see Schumpeter (1966)).

In relation to null jointness of factors of production, phases (2) and (4) are of interest. Note that if a factor combination $\{\nu_{k+1}, \nu_{k+2}, \ldots, \nu_n\}$, $(1 \leq k < n)$, is null joint with $\{\nu_1, \nu_2, \ldots, \nu_k\}$, for each positive bound $(x^o_{\nu_1}, x^o_{\nu_2}, \ldots, x^o_{\nu_k})$ on the subvector $(x_{\nu_1}, x_{\nu_2}, \ldots, x_{\nu_k})$, there is an input vector $x^o \varepsilon G := \{x \varepsilon R^n_+ : (x_{\nu_1}, x_{\nu_2}, \ldots, x_{\nu_k}) = (x^o_{\nu_1}, x^o_{\nu_2}, \ldots, x^o_{\nu_k})\}$ such that $\phi(x^o) = \max \{\phi(x) : x \varepsilon G\}$. This assertion is valid since the intersection $(\overline{C(1)} \cap G)$ is compact, ϕ upper semi-continuous and $\phi(x) = 0$ for $x \varepsilon (R^n_+ \setminus \overline{C(1)})$. From $\phi(x) = 0$ for $x\varepsilon(R^n_+ \setminus \overline{C(1)})$ it follows that for some $\bar{x}\varepsilon G$, $\phi(\bar{x}) = 0$. Therefore, both phase (2) and (4) are described in theorems (4.5.1) and (4.5.2). However, jointness of inputs does not imply that max $\{\phi(x): x\varepsilon G\} > 0$ for each positive bound $(x^o_{\nu_1}, x^o_{\nu_2}, \ldots, x^o_{\nu_k})$ on the subvector $(x_{\nu_1}, x_{\nu_2}, \ldots, x_{\nu_k})$, but property ϕ.4(a) guarantees the existence of such a maximum.

The first law of variable proportions, which is defined below, emphasizes phases (2) and (4).

(4.6.1) Definition: There is a Law of Variable Proportions for the factor combination $\{\nu_1, \nu_2, \ldots, \nu_k\}$, $(1 \leq k < n)$, if and only if there is an input vector $x^o \varepsilon OP(\nu_{k+1}, \nu_{k+2}, \ldots, \nu_n)$ such that $\phi(z^o) > 0$ for some $z^o := x^o - y^o$, where $y^o \varepsilon D(\nu_1, \nu_2, \ldots, \nu_k)$ and the set $S := (\{x\varepsilon R^n_+ : \|x\| > \|x^o\|\} \cap \{x\varepsilon R^n_+ : (x_{\nu_1}, x_{\nu_2}, \ldots, x_{\nu_k}) = (x^o_{\nu_1}, x^o_{\nu_2}, \ldots, x^o_{\nu_k})\})$ is contained in $OP(\nu_{k+1}, \nu_{k+2}, \ldots, \nu_n)$ and for each $\bar{x}^o \varepsilon S$, the function $\hat{\Phi}(\lambda) := \phi((1-\lambda)\cdot(\bar{x}^o_{\nu_1}, \bar{x}^o_{\nu_2}, \ldots, \bar{x}^o_{\nu_k}, 0, 0, \ldots, 0) + \lambda\cdot\bar{x}^o)$, $\lambda\varepsilon[0,1]$, has a maximum for some $\lambda^* \varepsilon[0,1]$ and $\hat{\Phi}(1) = 0$.

Note that if the factor combination $\{\nu_{k+1}, \nu_{k+2}, \ldots, \nu_n\}$ is essential, then $\hat{\Phi}(0) = 0$.

From theorems (4.5.1) and (4.5.2) the following characterization of the first law of variable proportions is clear.

(4.6.2) Theorem: Let the production structure satisfy ϕ.1-ϕ.5 in addition to ϕ.8 or being homothetic with $0 \varepsilon OP(\nu_{k+1}, \nu_{k+2}, \ldots, \nu_n)$. There is a law of variable proportions for the factor combination $\{\nu_1, \nu_2, \ldots, \nu_k\}$, $(1 \leq k < n)$, if and only if the factor combination $\{\nu_{k+1},\nu_{k+2},\ldots,\nu_n\}$ is null joint with $\{\nu_1,\nu_2,\ldots,\nu_k\}$.

In addition to definition (4.6.1) one can define a monotone law of variable proportions as:

(4.6.3) Definition: There is a Monotone Law of Variable Proportions for the factor combination $\{\nu_1,\nu_2,\ldots,\nu_k\}$, $(1\leqq k<n)$, if and only if there is an input vector $x^o \varepsilon OP(\nu_{k+1},\nu_{k+2},\ldots,\nu_n)$ such that $\phi(z^o) > 0$ for some $z^o := x^o - y^o$, where $y^o \varepsilon D(\nu_1,\nu_2,\ldots,\nu_k)$ and for each $\bar{x}^o \varepsilon(\{x\varepsilon R^n_+ : \| x \| > \| x^o \|\} \cap \{x\varepsilon R^n_+ : (x_{\nu_1},x_{\nu_2},\ldots,x_{\nu_k}) = (x^o_{\nu_1},x^o_{\nu_2},\ldots,x^o_{\nu_k})\})$ the function $\hat{\phi}(\lambda) := \phi((1-\lambda)\cdot(\bar{x}^o_{\nu_1},\bar{x}^o_{\nu_2},\ldots,\bar{x}^o_k,0,0,\ldots,0) + \lambda\cdot\bar{x}^o)$, $\lambda\varepsilon[0,1]$, has a maximum for some $\lambda^*\varepsilon[0,1]$, it is nondecreasing for $\lambda\varepsilon[0,\lambda^*]$, nonincreasing for $\lambda\varepsilon[\lambda^*,1]$ and $\hat{\phi}(1) = 0$.

From theorem (4.5.1) and the fact that $\hat{\phi}$ is quasi-concave if the production structure satisfies $\phi.8$ (see (6.B.15)), the following theorem follows:

(4.6.4) Theorem: Let the production structure satisfy $\phi.1$-$\phi.5$ and $\phi.8$. There is a monotone law of variable proportions for the factor combination $\{\nu_1,\nu_2,\ldots,\nu_k\}$, $(1\leqq k<n)$, if and only if the factor combination $\{\nu_{k+1},\nu_{k+2},\ldots,\nu_n\}$ is null joint with $\{\nu_1,\nu_2,\ldots,\nu_k\}$.

In order to elucidate the laws of variable proportions some two-input examples of the monotone law will be given.

As was pointed out above, if the factor combination $\{\nu_{k+1},\nu_{k+2},\ldots,\nu_n\}$, $(1\leqq k<n)$, is essential, then $\hat{\phi}(0) = 0$. The following modified Leontief production function is an example.

(4.6.5) $\phi(x_1,x_2) := \min\{\max\{0, x_1 - x_2\}, x_2\}$

This function satisfies properties $\phi.1$-$\phi.5$ and $\phi.8$ of the production structure. Thus, the function $\hat{\phi}(\lambda)$ is quasi-concave. The second factor x_2 is essential and x_2 is null joint with x_1. For each $(x_1,x_2) \varepsilon \mathrm{OP}(2)$ with $x_1 > 0$, the function $\hat{\phi}(\lambda)$ has the classical property of $\hat{\phi}(0) = 0$. It achieves a positive maximum for some $\lambda^* \varepsilon (0,1)$ and $\hat{\phi}(1) = 0$. Also, for $\lambda \varepsilon [0,\lambda^*]$ the function is nondecreasing and for $\lambda \varepsilon [\lambda^*,1]$ it is nonincreasing.

Modify the function (4.6.5) to read:

(4.6.6) $\phi(x_1,x_2) := \min\{\max\{0, x_1 - x_2 - a\}, x_2\}, \; a > 0.$

Again, the production function obeys properties $\phi.1$-$\phi.5$ and $\phi.8$. The second factor is essential and null joint with the first. However, for $(x_1,x_2) \varepsilon \mathrm{OP}(2)$ with $x_1 \leqq a$, $\hat{\phi}(\lambda) = 0$ for all $\lambda \varepsilon [0,1]$.

Turning to the case of symmetric null jointness, one has:

(4.6.7) $\phi(x_1,x_2) := \min\{\max\{0, x_1 - \tfrac{1}{2}\cdot x_2\}, \max\{0, x_2 - \tfrac{1}{2}\cdot x_1\}\}.$

This function satisfies $\phi.1$-$\phi.5$ and $\phi.8$, in addition of having x_1 and x_2 symmetric null joint. In this case, for each $(x_1,x_2) \varepsilon \mathrm{OP}(2)$ with $x_1 > 0$, $\hat{\phi}(0) = 0$, $\hat{\phi}(1) = 0$ with the existence of a $\lambda^* \varepsilon [0,1]$ such that $\hat{\phi}(\lambda^*) = \max\{\hat{\phi}(\lambda) : \lambda \varepsilon [0,1]\} > 0$. However, there is a $\lambda \varepsilon (0,1)$ such that $\hat{\phi}(\lambda) = 0$ for all $\lambda \varepsilon [0,\lambda)$, showing that for positive output x_2 must also be positive.

Next, consider the WDI function

$$(4.6.8) \quad \phi(x_1,x_2) = \begin{cases} A\cdot[\delta\cdot(x_1 - \tfrac{1}{2}\cdot x_2)^{-\rho} + (1-\delta)\cdot x_2^{-\rho}]^{-1/\rho} \\ \text{if } (x_1 - \tfrac{1}{2}\cdot x_2) \geqq 0 \\ 0 \text{ otherwise,} \end{cases}$$

where $A > 0$, $\delta\varepsilon(0,1)$ and $\rho\varepsilon(-1,0)$. Here, x_2 is null joint with x_1, but not essential. Thus, for $(x_1,x_2)\varepsilon OP(2)$ with $x_1 > 0$, $\phi(0) > 0$. $\phi(1) = 0$ and $\phi(\lambda)$ has a maximum on the interval $[0,1]$.

A discontinuity feature is also modeled by (4.6.8). Let $(x_1,x_2) = (1,2)$, then for $\lambda\varepsilon[0,\frac{1}{2}]$, $\phi(\lambda) > 0$, but for $\lambda\varepsilon(\frac{1}{2},1]$, $\phi(\lambda) = 0$. Thus, with continuous increases in x_2, output may suddenly become zero.

4.7 An Empirical Example of Congested and Null Joint Factors of Production

Agriculture is one of the many areas in which the ideas presented in this chapter can be applied. It is common knowledge that application of too much fertilizer can result in no yield. Experimental agricultural stations generate data for both the efficient and inefficient phases of the production structure, which are useful for testing production theory.

In an econometric study of corn growth (see Färe and Jansson, 1974:b) experimental data on output, (i.e., bushels of corn), and inputs (water irrigation (x_1) and nitrogen fertilizer (x_2)), were used to study null jointness and congestion. The input and output data were given for a fixed plot of land. Inspection of the data indicated that for proportional increases in water irrigation and fertilizer, the corn yield tended to decrease. Also, the data indicated that if x_1 was kept constant, output tended to decrease with large increases in fertilizer. These observations were used in fitting a three-input WDI production function to the data. The function chosen was

$$(4.7.1) \quad u = \begin{cases} A\cdot[\delta_1\cdot x_1^{-\rho}+\delta_2\cdot x_2^{-\rho}+(1-\delta_1-\delta_2)\cdot(x_3-\beta_1\cdot x_1-\beta_2\cdot x_2)^{-\rho}]^{-1/\rho} \\ \text{if } (x_3 - \beta_1\cdot x_1-\beta_2\cdot x_2) \geqq 0 \\ 0 \text{ otherwise} \end{cases}$$

The parameters were restricted by: $A > 0$, $\sum_{i=1}^{2} \delta_i$, $\delta_i \; \varepsilon[0, 1]$, $i = 1,2$, $\beta_i \varepsilon[0, +\infty)$, $i = 1,2$, $\rho\varepsilon(-1, +\infty)$. This function satisfies $\phi.1$-$\phi.5$, $\phi.8$, and is homogeneous of degree +1 in (x_1,x_2,x_3). x_3 denoted the fixed plot of land and was set equal to one.

A nonlinear optimization program was used to estimate the parameters of the production function (4.7.1) for each of four families of observations. The results were:

	1	2	3	4
A	1.15	1.30	1.23	1.23
	(0.04)	(0.05)	(0.05)	(0.04)
ρ	5.10	4,68	2,80	0,269
	(2.31)	(1,94)	(0.89)	(0.500)
δ_1	0.934	0.818	0.446	0.541
	(0.062)	(0.131)	(0.097)	(0.087)
δ_2	0.0141	0.0375	0.0812	0.192
	(0.258)	(0.0441)	(0.05600)	(0.054)
β_1	0.0	0.0	0.0	0.258
	(0.3)	(0.5)	(0.11)	(0.133)
β_2	0.229	0.226	0.087	0.240
	(0.033)	(0.076)	(0.140)	(0.071)
$\bar{R}^2$	0.935	0.916	0.947	0.952

For regressions 1,2 and 3, β_1 is not significantly different from zero, a result that is unsatisfactory, since excessive water should decrease output. A possible explanation of this is that the experiments were not undertaken with sufficiently large amounts of water, leading to too few inefficient observations. The same argument holds for fertilizer in the third regression.

On the other hand, regression 4 gave both β_1 and $\beta_2 > 0$ implying the possibility of overwatering and overfertilizing. This result is reasonable. It shows that the factor combination $\{x_1, x_2\}$ is null joint with x_1 and therefore OP- congested for some $x \varepsilon R^3_+$.

A final observation is that $\overline{R}^2$, the percentage variance explained by the regression and corrected for degrees of freedom, is high for all four regressions.

A schematic figure over the production function (4.7.1) with the parameters given by regression four is shown below.

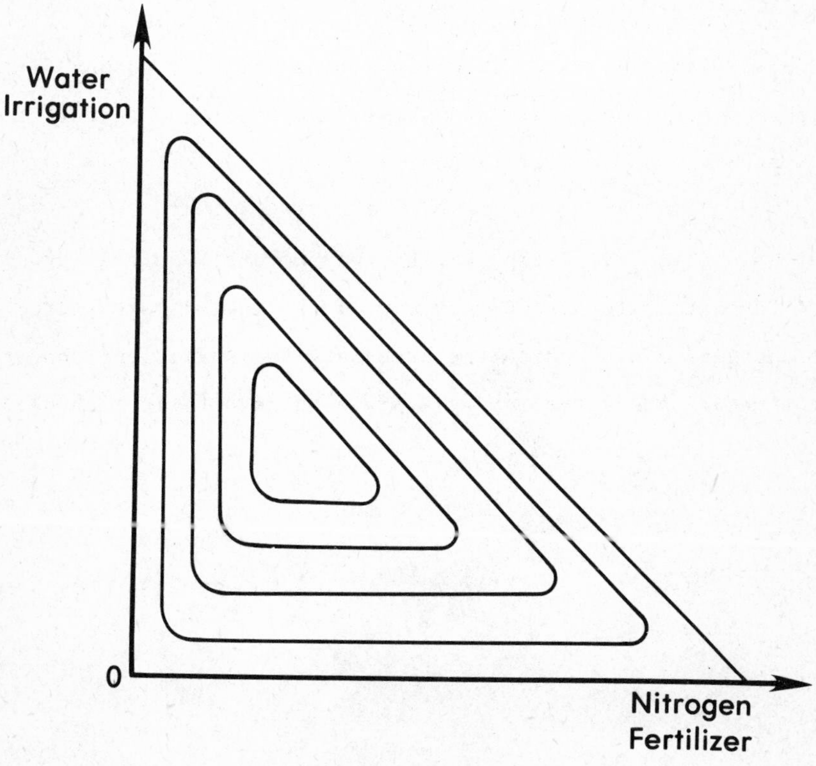

Figure 4.7.1
Isoquants for fixed land

5. THE LAW OF DIMINISHING RETURNS AT THE EXTENSIVE MARGIN

5.1 Introduction

The law of diminishing returns at the extensive margin, or as it will be referred to here, for extensive use of a factor, emerged from historical trends in agriculture (Steuart, 1767). As additional land opened up for cultivation, it was observed that relatively more land than before was required for proportional increases in yield (other factors increasing proportionally). Land opened up last was of poorer quality than that already in use.

This short chapter is devoted to a theoretical treatment of this law. In section 5.2 the law is defined for a two-input one-output production technology. A necessary and sufficient condition on this technology is proved for the law to apply.

In section 5.3, the properties of the two factors required for diminishing returns to extensive use of one of the factors are stated. These properties are based on the necessary and sufficient condition from section 5.2 and a theorem by R. Sato on holothetic technologies.

5.2 Diminishing Returns to Extensive Use of a Production Factor

In this section, a characterization of a two-input, one-output production structure exhibiting diminishing returns to extensive use of one of the factors of production is proved.

For this case, the law can be stated as follows: given increases in one factor, proportionally more of the other factor must be applied to increase output proportionally. A simple example ellucidates this idea. Let the production technology be given by the following almost homogeneous Leontief production function.

(5.2.1) $\phi(x_1, x_2) := \min \{x_1, \sqrt{x_2}\}$.

Here, for proportional increases in inputs, output will increase less than proportionally. However, if x_1 is increased by λ and x_2 by λ^2, $\lambda \geqq 1$, output will increase by λ. Hence, for proportional increases in output, proportionally more of the second factor is required. To formalize this production law, introduce:

(5.2.2) Definition: Let the production structure satisfy axioms $\phi.1$-$\phi.5$. If, for each $x \varepsilon R^2_+$ and $\lambda \geqq 1$ with $\phi(x) > 0$, there is a function $h(\lambda)$, which is bounded, and $h(\lambda) \geqq \lambda$, and there is a function $\Gamma(\lambda, \phi(x))$, compatible with the production axioms and $\Gamma(\lambda, \phi(x)) \geqq \lambda \cdot \phi(x)$ such that

(5.2.3) $\phi(\lambda \cdot x_1, h(\lambda) \cdot x_2) = \Gamma(\lambda, \phi(x_1, x_2))$,

then there are Diminishing Returns to Extensive Use of x_2.

This definition asserts that as x_1 is increased by λ and x_2 by not less than λ, output increases by at least λ. In order to characterize a subset of the technologies defined by (5.2.2) further assumptions are introduced. First, the functions h and Γ are assumed to be continuous and strictly increasing in λ, second, no factor is essential. For this subset of technologies one has:

(5.2.4) Theorem: Let ϕ, h and Γ satisfy the properties of definition (5.2.2). Assume that no factor is essential (see (3.2.2) for definition of essentiality) and that h and Γ are strictly increasing and continuous in λ. The most general production structure exhibiting diminishing returns to extensive use of x_2 is

$$\phi(\lambda\cdot x_1,\ \lambda^{\alpha}\cdot x_2) = F(\lambda\cdot\Omega(x_1,\ x_2)) = F(\Omega(\lambda\cdot x_1,\ \lambda^{\alpha}\cdot x_2)) \tag{5.2.5}$$

where $\alpha \geqq 1$. F is strictly increasing and continuous with $F(\lambda\cdot\Omega(x_1,\ x_2)) \geqq \lambda\cdot\phi(x_1,\ x_2)$ and $\Omega(x_1,\ x_2){:}= F^{-1}(\phi(x_1,\ x_2))$.

Proof: Since no factor is essential, there is an input vector $(x_1^0,0)\epsilon R_+^2$ such that $\phi(x_1^0,0) > 0$ (see property ϕ.4(a)). Let $\lambda,\ \mu > 1$, then from (5.2.3), note that by ϕ.1, $x_1^0 > 0$,

$$\phi(\lambda\cdot\mu\cdot x_1^0,0) = \Gamma(\lambda\cdot\mu,\phi(x_1^0,0)) = \Gamma(\lambda,\phi(\mu\cdot x_1^0,0)) = \Gamma(\lambda,\Gamma(\mu,\phi(x_1^0,0))).$$

Hence the function Γ satisfies the functional equation

$$\Gamma(\lambda\cdot\mu,\phi(x_1^o,0)) = \Gamma(\lambda,\Gamma(\mu,\phi(x_1^o,\ 0))). \tag{5.2.6}$$

In order to solve (5.2.6), define $F(\gamma){:}= \Gamma(\gamma,\phi(x_1^0,0))$, $\gamma > 0$. Then, F is strictly increasing and continuous, therefore,

$$(5.2.7) \quad \Gamma(\lambda,\phi(x_1^o,0)) = \Gamma(\lambda,F(F^{-1}(\phi(x_1^o,0)))).$$

Using (5.2.6), (5.2.7) and the definition of F,

$$(5.2.8) \quad \Gamma(\lambda,\phi(x_1^o,0)) = \Gamma(\lambda,\Gamma(F^{-1}(\phi(x_1^o,0), \phi(x_1^o,0))))$$
$$= \Gamma(\lambda\cdot F^{-1}(\phi(x_1^o,0)), \phi(x_1^o,0))$$
$$= F(\lambda\cdot F^{-1}(\phi(x_1^o,0))),$$

hence $\phi(\lambda\cdot x_1^o,0) = F(\lambda\cdot F^{-1}(\phi(x_1^o,0)))$. Conversely, substituting this expression for $\Gamma(\lambda,\phi(x_1^o,0))$ into (5.2.6) shows that $\phi(\lambda\cdot x_1^o,0) = F(\lambda\cdot F^{-1}(\phi(x_1^o,0)))$ is the general solution to $\phi(\lambda\cdot x_1,0) = \Gamma(\lambda,\phi(x_1^o,0))$. However, since $F(\gamma) := \Gamma(\gamma,\phi(x_1^o,0)) = \Gamma(\gamma,\phi(x_1,x_2))$ for all $(x_1,x_2)\varepsilon R_+^2$ such that $\phi(x_1,x_2) = \phi(x_1^o,0)$,

$$(5.2.9) \quad \Gamma(\lambda,\phi(x_1,x_2)) = F(\lambda\cdot F^{-1}(\phi(x_1,x_2)))$$

is the general solution of Γ. The properties of F follow from those of Γ.

To continue the proof, choose $(0,x_2)\varepsilon R_+^2$ such that $\phi(0,x_2) > 0$, $x_2 > 0$, (see ϕ.1 and ϕ.4(a)) and let $\lambda > 1$. From (5.2.3) and (5.2.9) it follows that

$$(5.2.10) \quad \lambda\cdot F^{-1}(\phi(0,x_2)) = F^{-1}(\phi(0,h(\lambda)\cdot x_2)).$$

Let $\lambda := h^{-1}(\mu)$, then by (5.2.10),

$$(5.2.11) \quad h^{-1}(\mu)\cdot F^{-1}(\phi(0,x_2)) = F^{-1}(\phi(0, \mu\cdot x_2)).$$

Choose $\mu := \delta\cdot\rho$, then by (5.2.11),

$$(5.2.12)\quad h^{-1}(\delta\cdot\rho)\cdot F^{-1}(\phi(0,x_2)) = F^{-1}(\phi(0,\delta\cdot\rho\cdot x_2)) = h^{-1}(\delta)\cdot F^{-1}(\phi(0,\rho\cdot x_2)) = h^{-1}(\delta)\cdot h^{-1}(\rho)\cdot F^{-1}(\phi(0,x_2)).$$

Hence,

$$(5.2.13)\quad h^{-1}(\delta\cdot\rho) = h^{-1}(\delta)\cdot h^{-1}(\rho).$$

The most general solution to the Cauchy functional equation (5.2.13) is (see Aczél, 1966)

$$(5.2.14)\quad h^{-1}(\lambda) = \lambda^{1/\alpha}.$$

Therefore, from the requirement $h(\lambda) \geqq \lambda$, $\lambda \geqq 1$, the general solution of h is

$$(5.2.15)\quad h(\lambda) = \lambda^{\alpha},\ \alpha \geqq 1.$$

Defining $\Omega(x_1,x_2) := F^{-1}(\phi(x_1,x_2))$, (5.2.9) and (5.2.15) give the most general production structure satisfying the conditions of theorem (5.2.4).

QED.

It is clear from example (5.2.1) that the restrictions imposed on the production structure by the conditions in theorem (5.2.4) are strong. However, there is an ample supply of almost homothetic production structures satisfying them.

5.3 Holothetic Production Structure and Diminishing Returns to Extensive Use of a Production Factor

In the preceding section, a characterization was given of production structures which have diminishing returns to extensive use of a production factor. It was shown that the subclass of almost homothetic production structures with $\alpha_1 = 1$, $\alpha_2 \geqq 1$ and $F(\lambda\cdot\Omega(x_1,x_2)) \geqq \lambda\cdot\phi(x_1,x_2)$ is the only production structure (under the conditions of theorem (5.2.4)) which exhibits diminishing returns to extensive use of x_2.

Here a tentative property of x_2 is shown, yielding this type of diminishing returns. For this purpose introduce (in accordance with R. Sato (1976)) a Holothetic Technology.

"...when the total effect of a given type of technical progress is completely transformed into a scale effect of production without changing the shape of the isoquant map, then the production function is said to be holothetic under a given type of technical progress..."

Technical progress or technical change can be thought of as "quality" differences, since Sato deals with factors measured in efficiency units.

Consider now the two-input production structure (2.5.2) and assume that the "quality" functions or technical change function for each factor can be written as,

$$(5.3.1) \qquad X_1 := e^{t}\cdot x_1 \text{ and } X_2 := e^{\alpha\cdot t}\cdot x_2,\ t \geqq 0,$$

respectively, where X_i, $i = 1,2$, is the efficiency unit of the i:th factor. e^t and $e^{\alpha\cdot t}$ represent quality levels at t and $\alpha \geqq 1$. Then, from (5.2.5),

$$(5.3.2) \qquad u = F(\Omega(X_1,X_2)) = F(\Omega(e^t \cdot x_1,\ e^{\alpha \cdot t} \cdot x_2))$$
$$= F(e^t \cdot \Omega(x_1,x_2))$$
$$= F_{(t)}(\Omega(x_1,x_2)).$$

Hence, the impact of the quality differences is transformed into scale effects. For each t, it is represented by another member of the same class of almost homothetic production structures.

In fact, by using Lie group theory, R. Sato (1976) proves for a production function twice continuously differentiable on the interior of R^2_+ that:

(5.3.3) Theorem: The class of production functions $\phi: R^2_+ \to R_+$, holothetic under biased factor-augmenting technical change, is the class of almost homothetic production technologies.

(For proof see R. Sato, 1976).

From theorem (5.3.3) by R. Sato and theorem (5.2.4) above, one can conclude that for a production structure $\phi: R^2_+ \to R_+$ twice continuously differentiable on the interior of R^2_+, satisfying the conditions of theorem (5.2.4), there are diminishing returns to extensive use of the second factor if and only if its quality is declining faster with increases in x_2 than that of the first factor.

6. STANDARD NOTATIONS AND MATHEMATICAL APPENDIX

6.A Some Standard Notations

$:=$	equal by definition.
$\backslash$	if A and B are sets, then $A\backslash B := \{a \in A : a \notin B\}$.
R_+	$R_+ :=$ {nonnegative real numbers}.
$u, v \in R_+$	u and v are outputs.
R_+^n	$R_+^n := R_+ \times R_+ \times \ldots \times R_+$.
$x, y, z \in R_+^n$	x,y and z are inputs.
$\geqq$	$x, y \in R_+^n$, $x \geqq y$ means x is not less than y.
$\geq$	$x, y \in R_+^n$, $x \geq y$ means $x \geqq y$ but $x \neq y$.
$>$	$x, y \in R_+^n$, $x > y$ means $x_i > y_i$, $i = 1,2,\ldots,n$.
$[a,b)$	$[a,b) := \{u \in R_+ : a \leqq u < b\}$.
$\| \; \|$	$\|x\| = (\sum_{i=1}^{n} x_i^2)^{\frac{1}{2}}$, Euclidean norm of $x \in R^n$.
$\| \; \|$	$\|u\|$ is the absolute value of $u \in R$.
$d(x,y)$	$d(x,y) := \|x - y\|$, the distance between x and y $x, y \in R_+^n$.

$s^\ell \to s^o$	the sequence s^ℓ converges to s^o, s^ℓ and $s^o \varepsilon R^n_+$.
$\limsup\limits_{x^\ell \to x} \phi(x^\ell)$	$\limsup\limits_{\ell \to +\infty} \phi(x^\ell) := \inf\limits_{\ell} \sup\limits_{k \geq \ell} \phi(x^k)$.
$\overline{A}$	closure of A.
$\overset{o}{A}$	interior of A.

6.B Mathematical Appendix

(6.B.1) Definition: A set $A \subset R_+^n$ is Bounded if and only if $d(x,y) := \sup\{d(x,y): x \varepsilon A, y \varepsilon A\} < +\infty$.

(6.B.2) Definition: A set $A \subset R_+^n$ is Compact if and only if it is closed and bounded or equivalently each sequence x^ℓ of A has a subsequence converging in A.

(6.B.3) Definition: A function $\phi: R_+^n \to R_+$ is Upper Semi-Continuous if and only if for each $x^o \varepsilon R_+^n$ and for each sequence $x^\ell \to x^o$, $\limsup_{\ell \to +\infty} \phi(x^\ell) \leqq \phi(x^o)$.

(6.B.4) Theorem: A function $\phi: R_+^n \to R_+$ is upper semi-continuous if and only if for each $u \varepsilon R_+$, the set $L(u) := \{x \varepsilon R_+^n: \phi(x) \geqq u\}$ is closed.

Proof: Let ϕ be upper semi-continuous and let x^o be a limit point of $L(u)$, $u \varepsilon R_+$. Let x^ℓ be an arbitrary sequence of $L(u)$, $x^\ell \to x^o$. Then

$$u \leqq \limsup_{\ell \to +\infty} \phi(x^\ell) \leqq \phi(x^o)$$

since ϕ is upper semi-continuous. Hence $x^o \varepsilon L(u)$ and $L(u)$ is closed.

Conversely, assume ϕ is not upper semi-continuous at $x^o \varepsilon R_+^n$. Then there is a sequence $x^\ell \to x^o$ such that $\limsup_{\ell \to +\infty} \phi(x^\ell) > \phi(x^o)$. Then for some $u \varepsilon R_+$, there is a subsequence x^{ℓ_k} of x^ℓ with $\lim_{k \to +\infty} \phi(x^{\ell_k}) = \limsup_{\ell \to +\infty} \phi(x^\ell) > u > \phi(x^o)$. Consequently, for some K, $\phi(x^{\ell_k}) > u$ for all $k \geqq K$ implying $x^{\ell_k} \varepsilon L(u)$ for all $k \geqq K$ but $x^{\ell_k} \to x^o \notin L(u)$. Hence $L(u)$ is not closed.

QED.

(6.B.5) Theorem: Let $\phi: R^n_+ \to R_+$ be upper semi-continuous and the set $A \subset R^n_+$ compact. Then, ϕ achieves a maximum on A.

Proof: Let $m = \sup\{\phi(x): x \in A\}$. There is a sequence x^ℓ of A such that $\phi(x^\ell) \to m$. Since A is compact there is a convergent subsequence $x^{\ell_k} \to x^0 \in A$. Clearly, $\phi(x^{\ell_k}) \to m$ and since ϕ is upper semi-continuous, $\phi(x^0) \geqq \lim_{k\to+\infty} \phi(x^{\ell_k}) = m$.

QED.

(6.B.6) Definition: A function $\phi: R^n_+ \to R_+$ is Continuous if and only if for each $x^0 \in R^n_+$ and for each $x^\ell \to x^0$, $\lim_{\ell\to+\infty} \phi(x^\ell) = \phi(x^0)$.

(6.B.7) Remarks: The function $\| \ \|$ is continuous. If ϕ is continuous, the sets $L(u): = \{x \in R^n_+: \phi(x) \geqq u\}$ and $\ell(u): = \{x \in R^n_+: \phi(x) \leqq u\}$ are closed and the set $L^0(u): = \{x \in R^n_+: \phi(x) > u\}$ is open. Proofs are obvious.

(6.B.8) Theorem: Let $\phi: R^n_+ \to R_+$ be continuous and let the set $A \subset R^n_+$ be compact. Then, ϕ achieves a maximum and a minimum on A.

Proof similar to proof of (6.B.4).

(6.B.9) Definition: $F: R_+ \to R_+$ is Strictly Increasing if and only if for $t^1 > t^0$, $F(t^1) > F(t^0)$.

(6.B.10) Theorem: Let $F: R_+ \to R_+$ be strictly increasing and continuous, then F has an inverse, strictly increasing and continuous.

Proof obvious.

(6.B.11) Theorem: Let $A \subset R^n_+$ be a closed set and let $x \varepsilon R^n_+$, $x \notin A$. Then $d(x,A) := \inf \{d(x,y): y \varepsilon A\} > 0$.

Proof obvious.

(6.B.12) Theorem: Let $A \subset R^n_+$, $x \varepsilon R^n_+$ then the function $f(x) := d(x,A)$ is continuous in $x \varepsilon R^n_+$.

Proof: Let $\varepsilon > 0$ and let x, $y \varepsilon R^n_+$ such that $d(x,y) \leqq \varepsilon$. There is an element $a \varepsilon A$ such that $d(x,a) \leqq d(x,A) + \varepsilon$. Therefore,

$$d(y,A) \leqq d(y,a) \leqq d(y,x) + d(x,a) \leqq d(x,A) + 2\varepsilon$$

and by symmetry,

$$| d(y,A) - d(x,A) | \leqq 2\varepsilon.$$

Hence, $f(x) := d(x,A)$ is continuous.

QED.

(6.B.13) Definition: A function $\phi: R^n_+ \to R_+$ is Quasi-Concave if and only if for each $x, y \varepsilon R^n_+$, $\phi((1-\delta)\cdot x + \delta\cdot y) \geqq \min \{\phi(x), \phi(y)\}$ for each $0 \leqq \delta \leqq 1$.

(6.B.14) Theorem: $\phi: R^n_+ \to R_+$ is quasi-concave if and only if $L(u) := \{x \varepsilon R^n_+ : \phi(x) \geqq u\}$, $u \varepsilon R_+$, is convex (i.e., for each $x, y \varepsilon L(u)$, $((1-\delta)\cdot x + \delta y) \varepsilon L(u)$, $0 \leqq \delta \leqq 1$).

Proof: Assume ϕ is quasi-concave. Then for any $u \varepsilon R_+$, let $x, y \varepsilon L(u)$ i.e., $\phi(x) \geqq u$. Hence $\phi((1-\delta)\cdot x + \delta\cdot y) \geqq \min \{\phi(x), \phi(y)\} \geqq u$, and $L(u)$ convex.

Conversely, suppose $L(u)$ convex $u \varepsilon R_+$. Let $x, y \varepsilon R^n_+$ and $\bar{u} = \min \{\phi(x), \phi(y)\}$. $L(\bar{u})$ convex implies $((1-\delta)\cdot x + \delta\cdot y) \varepsilon L(\bar{u})$, $0 \leqq \delta \leqq 1$. Hence, $\phi((1-\delta)\cdot x + \delta\cdot y) \geqq \bar{u} = \min \{\phi(x), \phi(y)\}$.

QED.

(6.B.15) Theorem: Let $A \subset R^n_+$ be a convex set, $\phi: R^n_+ \; R_+$, quasi-concave. Let $x, y \varepsilon A$ and define $\hat{\phi}(\delta) := \phi((1-\delta)\cdot x + \delta\cdot y)$, $0 \leqq \delta \leqq 1$. The function $\hat{\phi}$ is quasi-concave.

Proof obvious.

(6.B.16) Theorem (Hahn-Banach): Let $A, B \subset R^n_+$ be two non-empty disjoint convex sets. If A is compact and B closed there exists a hyperplane $H := \{x \varepsilon R^n_+ : \sum_{i=1}^{n} p_i \, x_i = \alpha, \; p \varepsilon R^n, \; \alpha \varepsilon R\}$, strictly separating A and B i.e.,

$$\sup \{ \sum_{i=1}^{n} p_i \cdot x_i : x \varepsilon B\} < \alpha < \inf \{ \sum_{i=1}^{n} p_i \cdot y_i : y \varepsilon A\}.$$

For proof see any book on convex analysis, e.g., Berge (1963).

(6.B.17) <u>Definition</u>: A function $\phi: R^n_+ \to R_+$ is concave if and only if for each x, $y \varepsilon R^n_+$, $\phi((1-\delta)\cdot x + \delta\cdot y) \geqq (1-\delta)\cdot\phi(x) + \delta\cdot\phi(y)$, for all $0 \leqq \delta \leqq 1$.

7. BIBLIOGRAPHY

ACZÉL, J. (1966): Lectures on Functional Equations and Their Applications. Academic Press, New York and London.

BERGE, C. (1963): Topological Spaces. Oliver and Boyd, Edinbrugh and London.

EICHHORN, W. (1978): Functional Equations in Economics. Addison-Wesley, Reading, Mass.

FÄRE, R. (1972): Strong Limitationality of Essential Proper Subsets of Factors of Production. Zeitschrift für Nationalökonomie 32, 417-424.

FÄRE, R. (1973): On Scaling Laws for Production Functions. Zeitschrift für Operations Research 17, 195-205.

FÄRE, R. (1978): A Dynamic Formulation of the Law of Diminishing Returns. Symposium on Production Theory, The Industrial Institute for Economic and Social Research, Stockholm.

FÄRE, R. and L. JANSSON (1974:a): Technological Change and Disposability of Inputs. Zeitschrift für Nationalökonomie 34, 283-290.

FÄRE, R. and L. JANSSON (1974:b): Estimation of Production Functions a Note, FOA rapport, C10005-M3 Stockholm.

FÄRE, R. and L. JANSSON (1975): On VES and WDI Production Functions. International Economic Review 16, 745-750.

FÄRE, R. and L. JANSSON (1976): Joint Inputs and the Law of Diminishing Returns. Zeitschrift für Nationalökonomie 36, 407-416.

FÄRE, R. and C.A.K. LOVELL (1979): Affinely Homothetic Production Technology. Department of Economics, Southern Illinois University, Carbondale, 79-01.

FÄRE, R. and R.W. SHEPHARD (1977): On Homothetic Scalar Valued Production Functions. The Scandinavian Journal of Economics 79, 131-132.

FÄRE, R. and L. SVENSSON (1979): Congestion of Production Factors. Department of Economics, Southern Illinois University, Carbondale, 79-04. To appear in Econometrica.

MENGER, K. (1936): Bemerkungen zu den Ertragsgesetzen. Zeitschrift für Nationalökonomie 7, 25-56. and: Weitere Bemerkungen zu den Ertragsgesetzen, ibid, 388-397. See also: The Logic of the Laws of Return, A Study in Metaeconomics, in: Economic Activity Analysis, ed. O. MORGENSTERN. New York (1954).

SATO, R. (1976): The Impact of Technical Change on the Holotheticity of Production Functions. Department of Economics, Brown University, Providence, Rhode Island, 76-11.

SCHUMPETER, J.A. (1966): History of Economic Analysis. Oxford.

SHEPHARD, R.W. (1953): Cost and Production Functions. Princeton University Press, Princeton.

SHEPHARD, R.W. (1967): The Notion of a Production Function. Unternehmensforschung 11, 209-232.

SHEPHARD, R.W. (1970:a): Theory of Cost and Production Functions. Princeton University Press, Princeton.

SHEPHARD, R.W. (1970:b): Proof of the Law of Diminishing Returns. Zeitschrift für Nationalökonomie 30, 7-34.

SHEPHARD, R.W. (1974): Semi-Homogeneous Production Functions and Scaling of Production. Lecture Notes in Economics and Mathematical Systems. Vol. 99. Springer-Verlag, Berlin.

SHEPHARD, R.W. and R. FÄRE (1974): The Law of Diminishing Returns. Zeitschrift für Nationalökonomie 34, 69-90.

SHEPHARD, R.W. and R. FÄRE (1978): Dynamic Theory of Production Correspondences, Part II. Operations Research Center, University of California, Berkeley, California, 78-3.

STEUART, J. (1767): see Schumpeter (1966).

TURGOT, A.R.J. (1767): Observations sur le Mémoire de M. Saint-Péravy 1767, in Oeuvres de Turgot, ed. Daire, Vol. 1, Paris, 418-483.

SUBJECT INDEX

Number underlined designates the page numbers on which the entry is defined.

Vol. 83: NTG/GI-Gesellschaft für Informatik, Nachrichtentechnische Gesellschaft. Fachtagung „Cognitive Verfahren und Systeme", Hamburg, 11.–13. April 1973. Herausgegeben im Auftrag der NTG/GI von Th. Einsele, W. Giloi und H.-H. Nagel. VIII, 373 Seiten. 1973.

Vol. 84: A. V. Balakrishnan, Stochastic Differential Systems I. Filtering and Control. A Function Space Approach. V, 252 pages. 1973.

Vol. 85: T. Page, Economics of Involuntary Transfers: A Unified Approach to Pollution and Congestion Externalities. XI, 159 pages. 1973.

Vol. 86: Symposium on the Theory of Scheduling and its Applications. Edited by S. E. Elmaghraby. VIII, 437 pages. 1973.

Vol. 87: G. F. Newell, Approximate Stochastic Behavior of n-Server Service Systems with Large n. VII, 118 pages. 1973.

Vol. 88: H. Steckhan, Güterströme in Netzen. VII, 134 Seiten. 1973.

Vol. 89: J. P. Wallace and A. Sherret, Estimation of Product. Attributes and Their Importances. V, 94 pages. 1973.

Vol. 90: J.-F. Richard, Posterior and Predictive Densities for Simultaneous Equation Models. VI, 226 pages. 1973.

Vol. 91: Th. Marschak and R. Selten, General Equilibrium with Price-Making Firms. XI, 246 pages. 1974.

Vol. 92: E. Dierker, Topological Methods in Walrasian Economics. IV, 130 pages. 1974.

Vol. 93: 4th IFAC/IFIP International Conference on Digital Computer Applications to Process Control, Part I. Zürich/Switzerland, March 19–22, 1974. Edited by M. Mansour and W. Schaufelberger. XVIII, 544 pages. 1974.

Vol. 94: 4th IFAC/IFIP International Conference on Digital Computer Applications to Process Control, Part II. Zürich/Switzerland, March 19–22, 1974. Edited by M. Mansour and W. Schaufelberger. XVIII, 546 pages. 1974.

Vol. 95: M. Zeleny, Linear Multiobjective Programming. X, 220 pages. 1974.

Vol. 96: O. Moeschlin, Zur Theorie von Neumannscher Wachstumsmodelle. XI, 115 Seiten. 1974.

Vol. 97: G. Schmidt, Über die Stabilität des einfachen Bedienungskanals. VII, 147 Seiten. 1974.

Vol. 98: Mathematical Methods in Queueing Theory. Proceedings 1973. Edited by A. B. Clarke. VII, 374 pages. 1974.

Vol. 99: Production Theory. Edited by W. Eichhorn, R. Henn, O. Opitz, and R. W. Shephard. VIII, 386 pages. 1974.

Vol. 100: B. S. Duran and P. L. Odell, Cluster Analysis. A Survey. VI, 137 pages. 1974.

Vol. 101: W. M. Wonham, Linear Multivariable Control. A Geometric Approach. X, 344 pages. 1974.

Vol. 102: Analyse Convexe et Ses Applications. Comptes Rendus, Janvier 1974. Edited by J.-P. Aubin. IV, 244 pages. 1974.

Vol. 103: D. E. Boyce, A. Farhi, R. Weischedel, Optimal Subset Selection. Multiple Regression, Interdependence and Optimal Network Algorithms. XIII, 187 pages. 1974.

Vol. 104: S. Fujino, A Neo-Keynesian Theory of Inflation and Economic Growth. V, 96 pages. 1974.

Vol. 105: Optimal Control Theory and its Applications. Part I. Proceedings 1973. Edited by B. J. Kirby. VI, 425 pages. 1974.

Vol. 106: Optimal Control Theory and its Applications. Part II. Proceedings 1973. Edited by B. J. Kirby. VI, 403 pages. 1974.

Vol. 107: Control Theory, Numerical Methods and Computer Systems Modeling. International Symposium, Rocquencourt, June 17–21, 1974. Edited by A. Bensoussan and J. L. Lions. VIII, 757 pages. 1975.

Vol. 108: F. Bauer et al., Supercritical Wing Sections II. A Handbook. V, 296 pages. 1975.

Vol. 109: R. von Randow, Introduction to the Theory of Matroids. IX, 102 pages. 1975.

Vol. 110: C. Striebel, Optimal Control of Discrete Time Stochastic Systems. III. 208 pages. 1975.

Vol. 111: Variable Structure Systems with Application to Economics and Biology. Proceedings 1974. Edited by A. Ruberti and R. R. Mohler. VI, 321 pages. 1975.

Vol. 112: J. Wilhelm, Objectives and Multi-Objective Decision Making Under Uncertainty. IV, 111 pages. 1975.

Vol. 113: G. A. Aschinger, Stabilitätsaussagen über Klassen von Matrizen mit verschwindenden Zeilensummen. V, 102 Seiten. 1975.

Vol. 114: G. Uebe, Produktionstheorie. XVII, 301 Seiten. 1976.

Vol. 115: Anderson et al., Foundations of System Theory: Finitary and Infinitary Conditions. VII, 93 pages. 1976

Vol. 116: K. Miyazawa, Input-Output Analysis and the Structure of Income Distribution. IX, 135 pages. 1976.

Vol. 117: Optimization and Operations Research. Proceedings 1975. Edited by W. Oettli and K. Ritter. IV, 316 pages. 1976.

Vol. 118: Traffic Equilibrium Methods, Proceedings 1974. Edited by M. A. Florian. XXIII, 432 pages. 1976.

Vol. 119: Inflation in Small Countries. Proceedings 1974. Edited by H. Frisch. VI, 356 pages. 1976.

Vol. 120: G. Hasenkamp, Specification and Estimation of Multiple-Output Production Functions. VII, 151 pages. 1976.

Vol. 121: J. W. Cohen, On Regenerative Processes in Queueing Theory. IX, 93 pages. 1976.

Vol. 122: M. S. Bazaraa, and C. M. Shetty, Foundations of Optimization VI. 193 pages. 1976

Vol. 123: Multiple Criteria Decision Making. Kyoto 1975. Edited by M. Zeleny. XXVII, 345 pages. 1976.

Vol. 124: M. J. Todd. The Computation of Fixed Points and Applications. VII, 129 pages. 1976.

Vol. 125: Karl C. Mosler. Optimale Transportnetze. Zur Bestimmung ihres kostengünstigsten Standorts bei gegebener Nachfrage. VI, 142 Seiten. 1976.

Vol. 126: Energy, Regional Science and Public Policy. Energy and Environment I. Proceedings 1975. Edited by M. Chatterji and P. Van Rompuy. VIII, 316 pages. 1976.

Vol. 127: Environment, Regional Science and Interregional Modeling. Energy and Environment II. Proceedings 1975. Edited by M. Chatterji and P. Van Rompuy. IX, 211 pages. 1976.

Vol. 128: Integer Programming and Related Areas. A Classified Bibliography. Edited by C. Kastning. XII, 495 pages. 1976.

Vol. 129: H.-J. Lüthi, Komplementaritäts- und Fixpunktalgorithmen in der mathematischen Programmierung. Spieltheorie und Ökonomie. VII, 145 Seiten. 1976.

Vol. 130: Multiple Criteria Decision Making, Jouy-en-Josas, France. Proceedings 1975. Edited by H. Thiriez and S. Zionts. VI, 409 pages. 1976.

Vol. 131: Mathematical Systems Theory. Proceedings 1975. Edited by G. Marchesini and S. K. Mitter. X, 408 pages. 1976.

Vol. 132: U. H. Funke, Mathematical Models in Marketing. A Collection of Abstracts. XX, 514 pages. 1976.

Vol. 133: Warsaw Fall Seminars in Mathematical Economics 1975. Edited by M. W. Loś, J. Loś, and A. Wieczorek. V. 159 pages. 1976.

Vol. 134: Computing Methods in Applied Sciences and Engineering. Proceedings 1975. VIII, 390 pages. 1976.

Vol. 135: H. Haga, A Disequilibrium – Equilibrium Model with Money and Bonds. A Keynesian – Walrasian Synthesis. VI, 119 pages. 1976.

Vol. 136: E. Kofler und G. Menges, Entscheidungen bei unvollständiger Information. XII, 357 Seiten. 1976.

Vol. 137: R. Wets, Grundlagen Konvexer Optimierung. VI, 146 Seiten. 1976.

Vol. 138: K. Okuguchi, Expectations and Stability in Oligopoly Models. VI, 103 pages. 1976.

Vol. 139: Production Theory and Its Applications. Proceedings. Edited by H. Albach and G. Bergendahl. VIII, 193 pages. 1977.

Vol. 140: W. Eichhorn and J. Voeller, Theory of the Price Index. Fisher's Test Approach and Generalizations. VII, 95 pages. 1976.

Vol. 141: Mathematical Economics and Game Theory. Essays in Honor of Oskar Morgenstern. Edited by R. Henn and O. Moeschlin. XIV, 703 pages. 1977.

Vol. 142: J. S. Lane, On Optimal Population Paths. V, 123 pages. 1977.

Vol. 143: B. Näslund, An Analysis of Economic Size Distributions. XV, 100 pages. 1977.

Vol. 144: Convex Analysis and Its Applications. Proceedings 1976. Edited by A. Auslender. VI, 219 pages. 1977.

Vol. 145: J. Rosenmüller, Extreme Games and Their Solutions. IV, 126 pages. 1977.

Vol. 146: In Search of Economic Indicators. Edited by W. H. Strigel. XVI, 198 pages. 1977.

Vol. 147: Resource Allocation and Division of Space. Proceedings. Edited by T. Fujii and R. Sato. VIII, 184 pages. 1977.

Vol. 148: C. E. Mandl, Simulationstechnik und Simulationsmodelle in den Sozial- und Wirtschaftswissenschaften. IX, 173 Seiten. 1977.

Vol. 149: Stationäre und schrumpfende Bevölkerungen: Demographisches Null- und Negativwachstum in Österreich. Herausgegeben von G. Feichtinger. VI, 262 Seiten. 1977.

Vol. 150: Bauer et al., Supercritical Wing Sections III. VI, 179 pages. 1977.

Vol. 151: C. A. Schneeweiß, Inventory-Production Theory. VI, 116 pages. 1977.

Vol. 152: Kirsch et al., Notwendige Optimalitätsbedingungen und ihre Anwendung. VI, 157 Seiten. 1978.

Vol. 153: Kombinatorische Entscheidungsprobleme: Methoden und Anwendungen. Herausgegeben von T. M. Liebling und M. Rössler. VIII, 206 Seiten. 1978.

Vol. 154: Problems and Instruments of Business Cycle Analysis. Proceedings 1977. Edited by W. H. Strigel. VI, 442 pages. 1978.

Vol. 155: Multiple Criteria Problem Solving. Proceedings 1977. Edited by S. Zionts. VIII, 567 pages. 1978.

Vol. 156: B. Näslund and B. Sellstedt, Neo-Ricardian Theory. With Applications to Some Current Economic Problems. VI, 165 pages. 1978.

Vol. 157: Optimization and Operations Research. Proceedings 1977. Edited by R. Henn, B. Korte, and W. Oettli. VI, 270 pages. 1978.

Vol. 158: L. J. Cherene, Set Valued Dynamical Systems and Economic Flow. VIII, 83 pages. 1978.

Vol. 159: Some Aspects of the Foundations of General Equilibrium Theory: The Posthumous Papers of Peter J. Kalman. Edited by J. Green. VI, 167 pages. 1978.

Vol. 160: Integer Programming and Related Areas. A Classified Bibliography. Edited by D. Hausmann. XIV, 314 pages. 1978.

Vol. 161: M. J. Beckmann, Rank in Organizations. VIII, 164 pages. 1978.

Vol. 162: Recent Developments in Variable Structure Systems, Economics and Biology. Proceedings 1977. Edited by R. R. Mohler and A. Ruberti. VI, 326 pages. 1978.

Vol. 163: G. Fandel, Optimale Entscheidungen in Organisationen. VI, 143 Seiten. 1979.

Vol. 164: C. L. Hwang and A. S. M. Masud, Multiple Objective Decision Making – Methods and Applications. A State-of-the-Art Survey. XII, 351 pages. 1979.

Vol. 165: A. Maravall, Identification in Dynamic Shock-Error Models. VIII, 158 pages. 1979.

Vol. 166: R. Cuninghame-Green, Minimax Algebra. XI, 258 pages. 1979.

Vol. 167: M. Faber, Introduction to Modern Austrian Capital Theory. X, 196 pages. 1979.

Vol. 168: Convex Analysis and Mathematical Economics. Proceedings 1978. Edited by J. Kriens. V, 136 pages. 1979.

Vol. 169: A. Rapoport et al., Coalition Formation by Sophisticated Players. VII, 170 pages. 1979.

Vol. 170: A. E. Roth, Axiomatic Models of Bargaining. V, 121 pages. 1979.

Vol. 171: G. F. Newell, Approximate Behavior of Tandem Queues. XI, 410 pages. 1979.

Vol. 172: K. Neumann and U. Steinhardt, GERT Networks and the Time-Oriented Evaluation of Projects. 268 pages. 1979.

Vol. 173: S. Erlander, Optimal Spatial Interaction and the Gravity Model. VII, 107 pages. 1980.

Vol. 174: Extremal Methods and Systems Analysis. Edited by A. V. Fiacco and K. O. Kortanek. XI, 545 pages. 1980.

Vol. 175: S. K. Srinivasan and R. Subramanian, Probabilistic Analysis of Redundant Systems. VII, 356 pages. 1980.

Vol. 176: R. Färe, Laws of Diminishing Returns. VIII, 97 pages. 1980.